KV-190-990

Internal Security Weapons & Equipment of the World

Internal Security
Weapons &
Equipment
of the World

Michael Dewar

LONDON

IAN ALLAN LTD

Contents

'We have seen in the last few years the growth of a cult of political violence, preached and practised not so much between states as within them. It is a sombre thought, but it may be that in the 1970s civil war, rather than war between nations, will be the main danger that we face.'

Mr Edward Heath, 1971

Half-title: *ITT IR torch shown fitted to NATO 7.62mm rifle in conjunction with an II weapon sight.*

First published 1979

ISBN 0 7110 0925 2

All rights reserved. No part of this book may be reproduced or transmitted in any form or by any means, electronic or mechanical, including photo-copying, recording or by any information storage and retrieval system, without permission from the Publisher in writing.

© Michael Dewar 1979

Published by Ian Allan Ltd, Shepperton, Surrey; and printed in the United Kingdom by Ian Allan Printing Ltd

Introduction

Internal Security Weapons & Equipment of the World contains full details of the important equipments designed exclusively or primarily for internal security (IS) situations in current use throughout the world. In addition, some of the many equipments that are still under development have been included to complete the picture.

Since World War II, governments throughout the world have had to face a greater degree of internal dissent, usually by a minority interest, than ever before. This has often taken the form of actual insurrection. The more recent phenomenon of international terrorism for political ends has only served to exacerbate the problem. In a rural environment it has usually been possible to adapt conventional equipment to meet this threat. In an urban environment however, most governments

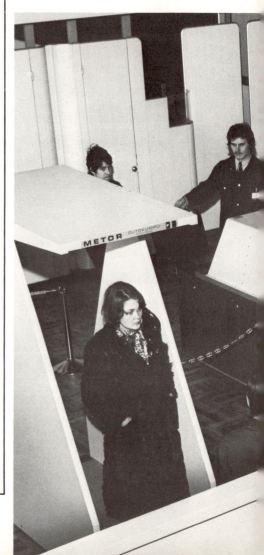

have found it to be both militarily sensible and politically expedient to develop or purchase special purpose IS equipment. It is therefore largely in the urban sense that the term Internal Security is used in this volume. In their widest sense IS operations include all operations undertaken by Government forces against indigenous armed groups that constitute a threat to the stability of the State.

It is not always easy to define IS equipment. Some equipment, such as that designed specifically for riot control — water cannons, riot guns, rubber bullets and the like — fall easily into the category. There are however twilight areas such as armoured vehicles, surveillance and communication equipments, weapon sights and some detection equipments, which could be fairly described as either IS or conventional military equipment depending on usage. The criteria used in this volume has been to establish if the equipment has been used in, or alternatively specifically manufactured for, an internal security situation.

The production of IS equipment is expanding to meet an ever increasing demand. There seems to be no limit to the inventiveness and ingenuity of security forces and of manufacturers to meet a complex and increasingly sophisticated threat. The range of IS equipment includes armoured vehicles, tear gas grenades and launchers, explosive and metal detectors, bomb disposal equipment, body armour and shields, and perimeter protection equipment. In addition, standard items of military equipment such as small arms and surveillance equipment play an important part.

In some countries the army is automatically called upon to deal with a riot. Elsewhere the police are used, and the army is only called in as a last resort. Many countries have formed special para-military organisations to deal with riots and other IS situations; examples are the Compagnie

Républicaine de Sécurité (CRS) in France, and the Federal Border Guard in the Federal Republic of Germany. This volume attempts to cover all types of IS equipment employed by these organisations throughout the world. Owing to the wide range of equipment involved, *Internal Security Weapons & Equipment of the World* is divided into sections, each reflecting a basic category of equipment.

The material in this volume has been supplied by various governments and manufacturers all over the world, and the author would like to express his thanks to all those who have assisted in its preparation. Because of the nature of the equipment, manufacturers have not always been at liberty to supply an exhaustive list of their customers, or a full specification of their equipment. Additional material, including photographs, for future editions of *Internal Security Weapons & Equipment of the World* should be forwarded to Ian Allan Ltd, Terminal House, Shepperton, TW17 8AS, England.

Michael Dewar
1978

Photo Credits

The photographs used to illustrate this book have been received from many companies, governments and individuals all over the world. The sources, where known, are listed below: Add-on Electronics Ltd (UK), Advanced Devices Laboratory (Belgium), AI Security Ltd (UK), Alsetex Company (France), Armour of America Ltd (USA), Associated Press, Balteau Company (Belgium), Barr & Stroud Ltd (UK), Berherman Demoen Company (Belgium), Berka Company (West Germany), Berliet Company (France), Bonaventure International Ltd (UK), Bristol Composite Materials Engineering Ltd (UK), Burlington Industrial Fabrics Co (USA), Cadillac Gage Co (USA), Calspan Technology Products Ltd (USA), Canadian Armed Forces, Chubb Security Systems Ltd (UK), Communications Control Incorporated (USA), Davin Optical Ltd (UK), Electron Company (West Germany), EMI Ltd (UK), Ericcson Telemateriel Company (Sweden), Euro-Med B V (Netherlands), Fabrique Nationale (Belgium), Fidelity Instrument Co Ltd (UK), French Embassy (London), Gault Glass Laminates Ltd (UK), GKN Sankey Ltd (UK), Glaverbel-Mécaniver (Belgium), Glover Webb & Liversidge Ltd (UK), Hi Spy Systems Ltd (UK), Institut Dr Forster (West Germany), International Air Radio Ltd (UK), International Defence Review (UK), ITT Electron Device Division (USA and UK), Israeli Embassy (London), Javelin Electronics Company (USA), J. Donne Holdings Ltd (UK, Jorgen Andersen Company (Denmark), Lawrence Scott & Electromotors Ltd (UK), Leigh Marsland Engineering Co Ltd (Canada), Marconi Elliott Engineering Co Ltd (UK), Marconi Elliott Mobile Radar Division (UK), Mauser Jagdwaffen GmbH (West Germany), Mercedes Benz (UK) Ltd, Ministry of the Interior (France), Mondart Enterprises Ltd (UK), Morfax Ltd (UK), Mossberg & Sons Inc (USA) Motorola Company (USA), Mowag AG (Switzerland), Omni Spectra Inc (USA), Outokumpu Oy Company (Finland), Pacemaker Press (Belfast), Panhard & Levassor (France), PDI Ltd (UK), Phillips Ltd (Netherlands), Pilkington Perkin Elmer (USA and UK), Plessey Company (UK), Popperfoto (London) Ltd, Press Association, Protective Materials Company (USA), P. W. Allen & Company (UK), Pye Dynamics Ltd (UK), Racal Amplivox Ltd (UK), Racal Tacticom Ltd (UK), Rank Telecommunications Ltd (UK), Remington Company (USA), Riwosa Company (Switzerland), Royal Small Arms Factory Enfield (UK), Saab Scania Company (Sweden), SAS Developments (UK), Saviem/Creusot-Loire (France), Schermuly Ltd (UK), Second Chance Body Armour (USA), Security Systems International (USA and UK), SEI (USA), Sherwood Company (USA), Shorrock Security Systems Ltd (UK), Short Brothers & Harland Ltd (UK), Sierra Engineering Company (USA), Smith & Wesson Company (USA, Tannoy Ltd (UK), Technology Investments Company (Eire), Thompson-CSF (France), Thyssen-Henschel Company (West Germany), Times Newspapers Ltd, Transvertex Company (Sweden), Trevor Davies Ltd (UK), United States Army, Vacuum Research Ltd (UK), Vallon Company (West Germany), Volumatic Ltd (UK), Webley Ltd (UK), W. S. Avery & Sons (UK).

Abbreviations

AP	Armour Piercing	IR	Infra Red
APC	Armoured Personnel Carrier	IS	Internal Security
AM	Amplitude Modulation	MG	Machine Gun
CCTV	Closed Circuit Television	MOD	Ministry of Defence
CRS	Compagnie Républicaine de Sécurité	MPCM	Multi Purpose Central Mount
DOV	Discreet Operations Vehicle	NOD	Night Observation Device
EOD	Explosive Ordnance Disposal	RF	Radio Frequency
EOR	Explosive Ordnance Reconnaissance	RX	Receiver
FM	Frequency Modulation	SA	Small Arms
GPMG	General Purpose Machine Gun	SWAT	Special Warfare Action Team
GRP	Glass Reinforced Plastic	TX	Transmitter
HF	High Frequency	UHF	Ultra High Frequency
IED	Improvised Explosive Device	VHF	Very High Frequency
II	Image Intensification		

Acknowledgements

The author would like to thank the following companies, organisations and individuals for their most valuable assistance during the preparation of this book:

Add-on Electronics Ltd (UK), Advanced Devices Laboratory (Belgium), AI Security Ltd (UK), Alsetex Company (France), Armour of America Ltd (USA), Balteau Company (Belgium), Barr & Stroud Ltd (UK), Berherman Demoen Company (Belgium), Berka Company (West Germany), Berliet Company (France), Bonaventure International Ltd (UK), Bristol Composite Materials Engineering Ltd (UK), Burlington Industrial Fabrics Co (USA), Cadillac Gage Co (USA), Calspan Technology Products Ltd (USA), Canadian Armed Forces, Chubb Security Systems Ltd (UK), Communications Control Incorporated (USA), Davin Optical Ltd (UK), Electron Company (West Germany), EMI Ltd (UK), Ericsson Telemateriel Company (Sweden), Euro-Med BV (Netherlands), Fabrique Nationale (Belgium), Fidelity Instrument Co Ltd (UK), French Embassy (London), Gault Glass Laminates Ltd (UK), GKN Sankey Ltd (UK), Glaverbel-Mécaniver (Belgium), Glover Webb & Liversidge Ltd (UK), Hi Spy Systems Ltd (UK), Institute Dr Forster (West Germany), International Air Radio Ltd (UK), International Defence Review (UK), ITT Electron Device Division (USA and UK), Israeli Embassy (London), Javelin Electronics Company (USA), J. Donne Holdings Ltd (UK), Jorgen Andersen Company (Denmark), Lawrence Scott & Electromotors Ltd (UK), Leigh Marsland Engineering Co Ltd (Canada), Marconi Elliot Avionics Systems Ltd (UK), Marconi Elliott Mobile Radar Division (UK), Mauser Jagdwaffen GmbH (West Germany), Mercedes Benz (UK) Ltd, Ministry of the Interior (France), Ministry of Defence (UK), Mondart Enterprises Ltd (UK), Morfax Ltd (UK), Mossberg & Sons Inc (USA), Motorola Company (USA), Mowag AG (Switzerland), Omni Spectra Inc (USA), Oto Melara Company (Italy), Outokumpu Oy Company (Finland), Panhard & Levassor (France), PDI Ltd (UK), Phillips Ltd (Netherlands), Pilkington Perkin Elmer (USA and UK), Plessey Company (UK), Protective Materials Company (USA), P. W. Allen & Company (UK), Pye Dynamics Ltd (UK), Racal Amplivox Ltd (UK), Racal Tacticom Ltd (UK), Rank Telecommunications Ltd (UK), Remington Company (USA), Riwosa Company (Switzerland), Royal Small Arms Factory Enfield (UK), Saab Scania Company (Sweden), SAS Developments (UK), Saviem/Creusot-Loire (France), Schermuly Ltd (UK), Second Chance Body Armour (USA), Security Systems International (USA and UK), SEI (USA), Sherwood Company (USA), Shorrock Security Systems Ltd (UK), Short Brothers & Harland Ltd (UK), Sierra Engineering Company (USA), Smith & Wesson Company (USA), Tannoy Ltd (UK), Technology Investments Company (Eire), Thompson-CSF (France), Thyssen-Henschel Company (West Germany), Transvertex Company (Sweden), Trevor Davies Ltd (UK), United States Army, Vacuum Research Ltd (UK), Vallon Company (West Germany), Volumatic Ltd (UK), Webley Ltd (UK), W. S. Avery & Sons (UK), Chris Donnelly (United Kingdom), Rupert Pengelly (United Kingdom), Judy Barclay (United Kingdom), Roger Stockton (United Kingdom).

A special word of thanks is due to the *International Defence Review* which provided much material and many photos. This magazine features IS equipment on a regular basis.

Section I: IS Vehicles

Today most armoured personnel carriers tend to be tracked. Tracked vehicles are not suited to the IS role for a number of reasons. They are difficult and expensive to operate and maintain, they are noisy, and most important of all, they are classed as 'tanks' by the layman. Use of 'tanks' in an IS situation is often politically unacceptable. Therefore most armoured IS vehicles are 4 x 4 wheeled vehicles which afford protection from small arms fire up to 7.62mm ball. Most IS vehicles are provided with observation blocks and firing ports. Vulnerable points on the vehicle such as the fuel tank and radiator must be given special protection, and the vehicle must be so designed as to allow rapid exit from and entry into the vehicle by the crew and passengers. IS armoured vehicles can be fitted with a variety of armaments including water cannon, tear gas launchers and machine guns. In addition to armoured vehicles there are a number of other types of vehicle that are commonly used in IS situations. These include water cannon vehicles, which may or may not be armoured, conventional 'soft skin' vehicles that have been covered in a composite lightweight armour and armoured bulldozers for the removal of barricades.

A recent innovation is the introduction of the Discreet Operational Vehicle (DOV). These are standard commercial vehicles and limousines that are armoured without appearing to be so. They are less provocative for low and medium risk IS incidents than the more heavily armoured, obviously military IS vehicles of the APC type or the para-military hydrid of the sort provided by Shorts or Glover-Hamble in the United Kingdom. There will continue to be IS situations that warrant the use of obviously military vehicles, but in many cases DOVs can be more politic and as effective. Incidents involving lightly armed terrorists, demonstrations and the safe conduct of VIPs are obvious examples.

It is not the intention of this section to duplicate the information in *Armoured Fighting Vehicles of the World* by Christopher Foss. Where information is duplicated it is solely to emphasise the IS role of that vehicle.

FN 4RM/62 Armoured Car

Belgium

Length: 4.5m
Width: 2.26m
Height: 2.37m
Ground Clearance: .324m
Wheelbase: 2.45m
Weight: 8,660kg
Engine: 4,750cc 6-cylinder FN-652 petrol developing 130hp at 3,500rpm
Crew: 3
No of Wheels: 4 x 4
Speed: 107kph
Range: 550-600km
Armament: 2 x FN MAG 7.62mm MG, 60mm breech loading mortar, 12 x smoke bomb launchers, *or* CATI 90mm gun, 1 x 7.62mm MG (externally mounted)

Development

FN of Herstal designed and manufactured the FN 4RM/62 in the early 1960s. The first prototype was built in 1962, the second in 1965 and production ended in 1971 when the 62 ordered by the Belgian Gendarmerie had been completed. The vehicle used many of the components of the 1.5-tonne (4 x 4) FN 4RM/62 Ardennes light truck and the engine of the 3.5-tonne 4 x 4 FN 4RM/652-3M medium truck (see pp 17-18 *Military Vehicles of the World*). The FAB is particularly suited to urban operations, alternative armament packages being available, both of which are mounted in a fully rotating turret.

Variants

A personnel carrier designed to carry eight men did not get beyond the prototype stage.

Employment

Belgian Gendarmerie.

Right: The FN 4RM/62 armoured car was developed for the Belgian Gendarmerie.

Engesa EE-II Urutu APC

Length: 6m
Width: 2.59m
Height: 2.09m (to hull roof)
Ground Clearance: .375m
Wheeltrack: 2.1m
Wheelbase: 3.05m
Weight: 11,000kg (unladen)
13,000kg (laden)
Engine: Diesel Mercedes-Benz OM-352A,
6-cylinder in line developing 174hp at 2,800rpm
Crew: 15
No of Wheels: 6 ×6
Speed: 95kph
Range: 600km
Gradient: 65%
Vertical Obstacle: .6m
Fording Depth: Amphibious
Turning Radius: 7.7m
Max Side Slope: 30%
Armament: Cupola for .50cal MG *or* 20mm
automatic gun and turret *or* 60mm gun mortar and
turret *or* 90mm cannon with coaxial 7.62mm NATO
MG and turret

Development

The EE-II Urutu has been designed and built by
Engesa of Sao Paulo, Brazil. It is an armoured
amphibious vehicle which has been designed to
perform various roles, and which can be transformed
into a family of vehicles. The engine of the Urutu is at
the front on the right of the driver which leaves the
rear of the hull free for a compartment capable of
accommodating up to 14 men or carrying 1,800kg
of cargo. A large door in the rear of the hull as well as
a door in either side provide excellent alternative
means of entry or exit. There are also four hatches in
the rear compartment in addition to the driver's
hatch. The vehicle is fitted with firing ports. The
engine air louvres can be closed to eliminate the risk
of flames from Molotov cocktails entering the engine
compartment, and cooling air is then admitted into
the engine from the crew compartment through a
pneumatically operated hatch which is normally
closed.

Variants

The design of the Urutu allows it to be transformed
into a family of vehicles. In addition to the APC
version, the Urutu can be used as an armoured
ambulance, a command and communication vehicle,
and an armoured cargo vehicle. The Engesa EE-9
Cascavel is an armoured car variant of the Urutu. The
overall specification of the Cascavel is similar, the
main differences being its turret mounted 90mm gun
and the fact that it is not amphibious, although it has
a fording capability of one metre.

Employment

Brazilian Army and Marines.

Below: *The Engesa Urutu showing its paces.*

Tatra OT64 APC

Czechoslovakia

Length: 7.468m
Width: 2.515m
Height: 2.235m
Ground Clearance: .381m
Weight: 14,515kg (laden)
Engine: Tatra T-928-14 V-8 diesel developing 300bhp at 2,000rpm
Crew: 20
No of Wheels: 8 x 8
Speed: 90kph
Range: 650km
Gradient: 60%
Vertical Obstacle: .5m
Fording Depth: Swims

Development

The OT-64 is based on the Tatra 815 truck, development of which started in 1959. The passengers, protected by 10mm of armour, are situated at the rear of the vehicle and are provided with overhead hatches, rear exit doors, and firing ports.

Variants

Variants include the Model 1 (7.62mm MG in an unprotected mount), Model 2 (12.7mm or 7.62mm MG with curved shield), Model 3 (14.5mm and 7.62mm MGs in an armoured turret), Model 4 (same armament as Model 3 but with a higher turret), Model 5 (the Model 1 with two Sagger anti-tank missiles mounted over the rear of the passenger compartment), and lastly the two command models, the R2 and R3.

Employment

Czechoslovakia, Egypt, Hungary, India, Libya, Morocco, Poland, Sudan, Syria, Uganda.

Walid APC

Egypt

Engine: German Deutz air-cooled engine
Crew: 10
No of Wheels: 4 x 4
Armament: Normally armed with a Goryunov SGM 7.62mm MG

Development

The Egyptians use the Walid open-top 4 x4, which is produced in Egypt, alongside their Soviet supplied equipments such as the BTR-152.

Employment

Egyptian, Algerian, Yemeni and Israeli armies.

Right: Designed and developed in Egypt, the Walid is used for police and military work.

Timoney BDX IS Vehicle

Eire

Length: 4.95m
Width: 2.41m
Height: 2.13m (to hull roof)
Ground Clearance: .38m
Wheeltrack: 1.9m
Wheelbase: 2.85m
Weight: ± 8,250kg (unladen), ± 9,350kg (laden)
Engine: Chrysler 360 CID V-8 spark ignition developing 200bhp at 4,000rpm
Crew: 12
No of Wheels: 4 x 4
Speed: 100kph
Range: 640-960km
Gradient: 60%
Vertical Obstacle: .4m
Fording Depth: Swims
Turning Radius: 14m
Max Side Slope: 45%

Armament: 7.62mm L37, L7 or L8 GPMG *or* .50 (12.7mm) Browning MG *or* 7.62mm MG MAG *or* Twin 7.62 MG MAG *or* 81mm mortar

Development

Design studies for the Timoney IS vehicle were started in January 1972 by the Irish Company Technology Investments Ltd (TIL), primarily to the specifications of the Irish Department of Defence. Nevertheless the first prototype was completed in July 1973 and two more prototypes were built by mid-1974. These three prototypes successfully concluded an exhaustive evaluation programme, and as a result TIL is now building a first batch of pre-production vehicles. A production licence has also been taken out by the Belgian Company Beherman Demoen of Bornem, hence the designation BDX. The vehicle is designed primarily for an urban combat

Left: *The Timoney BDX.*

situation, but is also able to perform more conventional military duties in a rural environment. Its 12.5mm armour is thicker than on most other vehicles of its kind, and provides protection against 7.62mm armour-piercing bullets fired at short range, yet does not involve excessive weight. The driver is seated well forward to give him the widest possible field of view and has a large windscreen of laminated glass possessing the same strength as the vehicle body, with two smaller side windows of the same material. The provision of these relatively large windows meets the need for good vision from within an armoured vehicle in urban operations. Doors in either side, as well as in the rear of the hull, meet the third requirement for urban operations, namely the provision of multiple means of entry or exit.

Variants

The design lends itself to the production of a variety of vehicle types, including six and eight-wheel vehicles, having a high degree of component interchangeability. Studies are underway to look at a turreted armoured reconnaissance vehicle, a six-wheeled APC, and an unarmoured amphibious load carrier. The existing BDX has a variety of turret options, and can be fitted with a dozer blade for clearing barricades.

Employment

Irish Army, Belgian Gendarmerie, Belgian Air Force. Negotiations are currently in hand with one other European government and with one African country.

Berliet VXB 'Gendarmerie' IS Vehicle   France

Length: 5.9m
Width: 2.44m
Height: 2.05m
Ground Clearance: .38m
Wheeltrack: 2.04m
Wheelbase: 3m
Weight: 8,900kg (unladen)
12,000kg (laden)
Engine: Berliet diesel engine developing 170hp
Crew: 15
No of Wheels: 4 x 4
Speed: 85kph
Range: 750km

Gradient: 60%
Fording Depth: Swims
Turning Radius: 15.6m
Armament: Externally mounted 7.5 or 7.62mm MG

Development

The VXB 'Gendarmerie' is designed to meet the particular requirements of police armoured units, and has been in production at Berliet's Bourg factory

Below: *Berliet VXB 170 'Gendarmerie'.*

since 1973. The characteristics which make the VXB 'Gendarmerie' ideal for IS missions include the large crew compartment of 11 cubic metres, the excellent visibility with no blind spots (the windows are bullet proof glass reinforced with steel mesh), easy entry and exit (two large doors in the sides and one at the rear), effective protection against small arms fire, mines and bombs (engine air intakes can be blocked), and good manoeuvrability. One VXB prototype was fitted with the TOP7 commander's cupola of the AMX 30 battle tank, one of the best observation cupolas available. To date customers have found this option too expensive, but its experimental installation illustrates the importance given to vision in the VXB anti-riot vehicle.

Variants

The VXB 'Combat' is designed to meet the requirements of modern armoured units and can mount a wide range of armaments. The VXB 'Gendarmerie' may be equipped with a dozer blade and/or a hydraulic winch.

Employment

French Gendarmerie, and armed forces of Gabon, Tunisia and Senegal.

Ford (France) IS Reconnaissance Vehicle   France

Development

The Ford Transit has been transformed by the CRS into an IS Reconnaissance Vehicle carrying nine riot police. It is equipped with radio, a public address system, and anti-riot grills. It is used to transport a quick reaction force in urban areas.

Employment

French CRS.

Right: *Ford (France) Transit adapted by French CRS as reconnaissance vehicle.*

Panhard AML H60-7 Armoured Car (IS Version)   France

Length: 3.79m
Width: 1.97m
Height: 1.86m (to turret roof)
Ground Clearance: .305m
Wheeltrack: 2.05m
Wheelbase: 2.7m
Weight: 4,800kg
Engine: Panhard 4HD 4-cylinder 1,997cc 90hp
Crew: 3
No of Wheels: 4 x 4
Speed: 90kph
Range: 600km
Gradient: 60%
Fording Depth: 1.10m
Turning Radius: 13.1m
Max Side Slope: 30%
Armament: One 60mm CMA1 Hotchkiss Brandt Gun/Mortar breech or muzzle loaded and two AA-52 NF-1 or MAG-80 7.62mm MG

Right: *The Panhard AML armoured car in its 60-7HB version is a good example of an armoured vehicle specifically designed for anti-guerilla operations and the protection of lines of communication.*

Development

Development of the AML series started in 1956. The wide range of possible armaments, the good performance and low operating cost (the Panhard 4HD engine does 100km on about 26 litres) have made the AML particularly appreciated by those countries with a restricted military budget. The H600-7 version has been specially designed for IS and anti-guerilla operations, and for use in built-up areas.

Variants

AMH 90 Reconnaissance Vehicle mounting a 90mm gun. AML 60/20 Reconnaissance Vehicle mounting a 60mm mortar and a 20mm cannon.

Employment

4,000 AMLs of all types have been produced, 700 for the French Army and Gendarmerie. The AML is also used by Algeria, Burundi, Cambodia, Congo, Ecuador, Eire, Ethiopia, Iraq, Israel, Ivory Coast, Kenya, Libya, Mauritania, Morocco, Malaysia, Nigeria, Portugal, Rhodesia, Rwanda, Saudi Arabia, Senegal, South Africa, Spain, Tunisia, Abu Dhabi, Chad, Upper Volta, Lebanon, Venezuela and Zaire.

Panhard M3 VTT APC   France

Length: 5.305m
Width: 2.5m
Height: 1.748m
Ground Clearance: .474m
Wheeltrack: 2.12m
Wheelbase: 2.95m
Weight: 5,800kg (laden)
Engine: Panhard 4HD 4-cylinder 1,997cc 90hp
Crew: 12
No of Wheels: 4 x 4
Speed: 90kph
Range: 600km
Gradient: 60%
Fording Depth: Swims
Turning Radius: 13.1m
Max Side Slope: 30%
Armament: Forward: One swivel mounted weapon support for 7.5 or 7.62mm AA-52 MG *or* TL2152 turret mounting two 7.62mm MG *or* T20 turret mounting one 20mm cannon and coaxial 7.62mm MG
Rear: One weapon support revolving on semi-circular rail for 7.5 or 7.62mm AA-52 MG or a MAG 80-MG.

Development

The M3 series was designed as a troop transport complement to the AML towards the end of the 1960s. In relation to the size of its hull the vehicle has an exceptional carrying capacity of 11 men plus the driver. The M3 uses 95 of the components of the AML, but has the additional advantage of being amphibious without preparation. Protection for the personnel on board, who can use their individual weapons through six side ports, and enter and exit through two large rear doors, is provided by 10mm armour plate and attention has also been given to protecting all apertures against the entry of inflammable liquids.

Variants

M3 VDA AA Weapon system, armament two HS 820 SL (or M693) 20mm cannons; M3 VTS Ambulance; M3 VPC Command Vehicle, armament as for VTT; M3 VAT Recovery Vehicle.

Panhard is also reported to have a new family of armoured vehicles of advanced design under development. Hydro-pneumatic suspension has been adopted, and the family will include 4 x4 and 6 x 6 models. An experimental 8 x 8 model has also been developed.

Employment

Abu Dhabi, Angola, Congo, Eire, France, Iraq, Kenya, Lebanon, Malaysia, Portugal, Saudi Arabia and Spain.

Left: *The Panhard M3 wheeled APC.*

Saviem S95 Command Vehicle   France

Development

Developed by Saviem, the S95 command vehicle is a good example of the type of police/para-military vehicle that is ideal for controlling complex urban situations involving the deployment of IS forces throughout a large urban area. The vehicle is equipped with radio telephone and radio communications facilities that permit control of a large number of sub-stations.

Employment

French CRS.

Left: *Saviem S95 police command vehicle.*

Saviem/Creusot-Loire VMO IS Vehicle   France

Length: 5.98m
Width: 2.5m
Height: 2.06m
Ground Clearance: .4m
Wheeltrack: 2.07m
Wheelbase: 3m
Weight: 10,900kg (unladen)
12,900-13,900kg (laden)
Engine: 235hp diesel
Crew: 12
No of Wheels: 4 x 4
Speed: 90kph

Range: 1,300km
Gradient: 50%
Fording Depth: Swims
Max Side Slope: 35%
Armament: TL1G light turret manufactured by Creusot-Loire situated centrally and mounting a 7.62mm MG and a 40mm grenade launcher

Development

Saviem in collaboration with Creusot-Loire (the two Companies formed the Société des Materiels Spéciaux Saviem-Creusot-Loire) produced the VAB,

Left: *Saviem/Creusot-Loire VMO IS vehicle showing dozer blade lowered.*

from which the VMO is derived, to meet a specification put out in 1969 by the French General Staff for a multi-role amphibious wheeled armoured vehicle to fill a forward tactical support role. The vehicle was adopted in mid-1974 by the French Army, which will be purchasing 4,000 over a 10-year period. The VMO is an IS variant of the VAB and first appeared in 1977. Illumination on the VMO is provided by a searchlight which pivots with the gun mounting. Optional equipment ·comprises a periscope (magnification x 1) linked to a retractable sight (magnification x 3), pivoting with the weapon mounting, plus four side observation periscopes. Weight of the turret including weapons, ammunition and optics is 270kg. An optional item of equipment is a hydraulically controlled dozer blade which enables the vehicle to breach road barricades etc.

Variants

The VAB is also produced in a 6 × 6 version and with a variety of armaments including HOT or TOW missiles, twin 20mm AA MG and 20 or 30mm cannon. Command and recovery variants are available.

Employment

French Army.

Mercedes-Benz Water Cannon Germany

Development

The Mercedes-Benz Water Cannon is a conventional Mercedes-Benz truck chassis with coachwork completed by Saval-Kronenberg of Hedel, also of West Germany. The vehicle is fitted with two powerful water-cannons, and a large quantitiy of water is carried in the rear.

Employment

West Berlin Police, several state police forces in West Germany, and British Army.

Below: *Mercedes-Benz water cannon.*

Rheinstahl UR416 APC (IS Version) Germany

Length: 5.2m
Width: 2.26m
Height: 1.24m
Ground Clearance: .44m
Wheeltrack: 1.616m
Wheelbase: 2.9m
Weight: 4,600kg (unladen)
6,300kg (laden)
Engine: 110hp 6-cylinder Daimler-Benz OM-32 water-cooled diesel
Crew: 10
No of Wheels: 4 × 4

Speed: 80kph
Range: 700km
Gradient: 70%
Vertical Obstacle: .55m
Fording Depth: 1.00m
Turning Radius: 12.9m
Armament: Externally mounted 7.62mm MG

Development

Development work on the UR416 started in 1965 when a prototype was produced, and it went into production in 1969 with Thyssen Maschinenbau of

Witten-Annen (formerly Rheinstahl and now Thyssen-Henschel). The UR416 is a light armoured vehicle produced expressly for IS and frontier patrol work. Although the designers used an existing chassis on which to base their vehicle, namely the 1.5-tonne Daimler-Benz UNIMOG S-404 light truck, it differs from most other vehicles of its type in having an armoured shell (6mm steel plate resistant to 7.62 AP projectiles) which can be very easily removed for mechanical repairs and servicing (see photo). The crew are transported sitting back-to-back, facing the observation/firing ports, and close to the three large exits. Visibility is good in front, where large windscreens are provided for the commander and driver. The vehicle also mounts a dozer blade and 'cow-catcher' for clearing barricades and other obstacles that are likely to be encountered in an urban IS situation.

Variants

Turret with either single or twin 7.6mm MG and three smoke dischargers mounted on each side; *or*

Above: A simple system of assembly allows the UR416 to be separated, within minutes, into its two major sub-assemblies: the armoured hull and the automotive assembly.

Turret mounting 20mm Rh 202 cannon; *or* Turret mounting 90mm MECAR assault gun; *or* Turret mounting COBRA or TOW guided weapons.

Thyssen-Henschel currently have under development a new 4 × 4 armoured car for IS use which will use the new Daimler-Benz UNIMOG U-120 light truck chassis.

Employment

The UR416 has had substantial export success, and of the 450 so far produced, 300 have gone to Peru, 20 to Venezuela, 30 to Togo, 20/30 to Kenya, 2 to Holland, 20 to El Salvador, 15 to Greece, 30 to Morocco, and 10 to the German Police. Interestingly 17 UNIMOG chassis with armoured shells produced in Sweden have been in service in the Irish Army since 1972.

Ramta RBY Mk 1 Patrol Vehicle   Israel

Length: 4.988m
Width: 2.03m
Height: 1.66m
Ground Clearance: .375m
Wheelbase: 3.4m
Weight: 3,600kg
Engine: Dodge 225-2 6-cylinder 120hp
Crew: 8

No of Wheels: 4 × 4
Speed: 100kph
Range: 550km
Fording Depth: 1.0m
Armament: The vehicle can be equipped with a wide range of weapons, including a 106mm recoiless rifle or twin 20mm AA guns, though its normal armament in its IS role is two 7.62mm MG

Left: *Ramta RBY Mk 1.*

Development

The Ramta is manufactured by Ramta Structures and Systems, which is a subsidiary of Israel Aircraft Industries Ltd of Beersheba. The Ramta RBY Mk I is particularly suitable for frontier and rural patrolling. It has an exceptional power to weight ratio ensuring good acceleration and a high top speed. Armour is 8mm thick and provides effective protection against close range small arms fire. The underside of the vehicle is 10mm steel plate, v-shaped to give maximum protection against mines.

Employment

Israeli Army.

Fiat 6614CM APC Italy

Length: 5.86m
Width: 2.5m
Height: 1.78m (to hull roof)
Ground Clearance: .37m
Wheeltrack: 1.96m
Wheelbase: 2.9m
Weight: 7,000kg (unladen)
8,500kg (laden)
Engine: Fiat 6-cylinder diesel developing 160hp at 3,200rpm
Crew: 11

No of Wheels: 4 x 4
Speed: 100kph
Range: 700km
Gradient: 60%
Vertical Obstacle: 45m
Fording Depth: Swims
Turning Radius: 7.96m
Max Side Slope: 30%
Armament: 12.7mm Browning M2 Heavy MG, 7.62mm MG

Left: *Like many vehicles designed with an eye to operations against urban guerillas, the Fiat 6614CM has doors in three positions for rapid egress.*

Development

The 6614CM APC and its companion vehicle, the 6616BM Armoured Car, are the first armoured vehicles to be built in Italy since the end of World War II. With a good performance, and both using the same mechanical components, these are relatively advanced vehicles without being too sophisticated. The aim is simplicity, reliability, safety and low cost. Firing ports are provided for individual weapons, and exit from the vehicle is reasonably simple through the large rear ramp and two side doors.

Variants

6616BM Armoured Car with revolving turret mounting a 20mm automatic cannon and coaxial 7.62mm MG, and a variable range smoke grenade launcher breech loaded from inside the turret, and six fixed range smoke grenade dischargers. Alternatively TOW or MILAN missiles can be fired from the turret.

Employment

Italian Army, Italian Carabinieri.

Police Anti-Riot Vehicle

Japan

A specification of this vehicle is not available. The vehicle was first seen in use in Tokyo in November 1971 manned by the Tokyo Police Department. The vehicle's equipment includes powerful water guns and searchlights. Side exits are provided.

Left: *Japanese police anti-riot vehicle shown in action in Tokyo in November 1971.*

Hippo Anti-Riot Vehicle

South Africa

Development

The Hippo Anti-Riot Vehicle has been built in South Africa specifically for use in riot situations. The crew and passengers are accommodated in a wedge-shaped upper compartment which is designed to deflect the blast from land mines upwards and sideways. The height of the crew and passenger compartment off the ground also affords a degree of protection against mines. The rear of the vehicle can accommodate approximately 10 men. A detailed specification of the Hippo is not available, but the vehicle is quite clearly a highly original approach to the mine threat. It also appears to be a useful, rugged and practical vehicle for riot situations.

Employment

South African Army and Police, Rhodesian Army and Police.

Right: *An African police constable stands by a police Hippo riot wagon.*

Mowag Grenadier IS Vehicle

Switzerland

Length: 4.9m
Width: 2.43m
Height: 1.75m (to hull roof)
Ground Clearance: .4m
Wheeltrack: 1.99m (front)
2m (rear)
Wheelbase: 2.5m
Weight: 5,000kg (unladen)
6,000kg (laden)
Engine: as for Roland
Crew: 8
No of Wheels: 4 x 4
Speed: 100kph
Range: 750km
Gradient: 70%
Vertical Obstacle: .4m
Fording Depth: Swims (employs propeller drive)

Turning Radius: 12.9m
Max Side Slope: 30%
Armament: As for Roland, but in addition can mount 25mm Oerlikon cannon

Development
The Grenadier was developed by Mowag to fill several roles including that of IS vehicle.
Variants
Also built without propeller drive.

Employment
Details not available.

Below: *Mowag Grenadier IS vehicle.*

Mowag Piranha IS Vehicle

Switzerland

Length: 5.39m
Width: 2.5m
Height: 1.85m (to hull roof)
Ground Clearance: .5m
Wheeltrack: 2.18m (front)
2.205m (rear)
Wheelbase: 2.5m
Weight: 5,850kg (unladen)
7,000kg (laden)
Engine: Petrol engine developing 235hp at 4,000rpm
Crew: 8
No of Wheels: 4 x 4
Speed: 100kph
Range: 750km

Gradient: 70%
Fording Depth: Swims
Turning Radius: 12.6m
Max Side Slope: 35%
Armament: Any calibre armament up to an Oerlikon 25mm automatic cannon

Development
The Piranha family of 4 x 4, 6 x 6 and 8 x 8 armoured vehicles represent Mowag's most recent designs. There are three different length hulls with 2, 3 and 4 axles accommodating 8,10 and 11 men respectively. For the IS role, the smaller and cheaper versions are obviously most suitable.

Variants

The ideas and concepts incorporated in the Piranha can be found in the Puma, a 6 × 6 vehicle with steering on both front and rear wheels. Completely amphibious and weighing 16,000kg in combat order, this vehicle is still at the prototype stage.

Above: Mowag Piranha wheeled 6×6 version suitable for IS duties.

Employment

Details not available.

Mowag Roland IS Vehicle   Switzerland

Length: 4.44m
Width: 2.01m
Height: 1.62m (to hull roof)
Ground Clearance: .4m
Wheeltrack: 1.7m (front)
1.66m (rear)
Wheelbase: 2.5m
Weight: 3,900kg (unladen)
4,700kg (laden)
Engine: Chrysler 8-cylinder developing 202hp at 3,900rpm
Crew: 7

No of Wheels: 4 × 4
Speed: 110kph
Range: 750km
Gradient: 70%
Vertical Obstacle: .4m
Fording Depth: 1.00m
Turning Radius: 12.9m
Max Side Slope: 30%

Below: Mowag Roland IS vehicle.

Armament: The standard armament is a small truncated cone turret armed with remotely controlled externally mounted 7.62mm MG (usually a SIG MG 710-3 or an FN MAG-80)

Development

The Roland was developed by Mowag of Kreuzlingen, Switzerland, and was designed to fill several roles including that of IS vehicle. An obstacle clearing blade can be fitted.

Variants

An amphibious version of Roland weighing 5,500kg (laden) with a slightly larger hull is able to float without preparation.

Employment

The Roland is in service with a number of countries including several in South America.

Mowag Wotan IS Vehicle   Switzerland

Length: 5.31m
Width: 2.2m
Height: 2.22m (to top of turret)
Ground Clearance: .5m
Wheeltrack: 1.95m
Wheelbase: 2.6m
Weight: 8,600kg
Engine: Chrysler R-319 6-cylinder petrol developing 161bhp
Crew: 7
No of Wheels: 4 x 4, steering on all 4
Speed: 85kph
Range: 400km
Gradient: 60%
Armament: Manually operated 7.6mm MG mounted externally

Development

The Wotan was first produced in 1957/8 and in 1959 20 were supplied to the German Frontier Police, who subsequently decided to equip all their mobile units with the vehicle. In 1962 Henschel (now Thyssen-Henschel) produced 260 under

Above: Mowag Wotan showing its paces in deep sand.

licence, most of them without armament and fitted only with an observation cupola for the vehicle commander, and designated the SW-1 KFz-91. A number were fitted with a turret mounting a 20mm Mk 20-1 (HS 820) cannon, and this version was designated the SW-II KFz-91.

Variants

Wotans vary only in their armament. The following are available: Mowag single place turret armed with an Oerlikon 5TG 20mm automatic cannon (model MR8-09); A turret armed with a 90mm gun (model MR8-23); Twin Oerlikon 80mm rocket launchers (model MR8-30) or a Tampella 120mm mortar (model MR8-32).

Employment

German Frontier Police, West German Police, Chile.

Alvis Saladin Mk 2 Armoured Car   UK

Length: 5.284m (including gun)
Width: 2.54m
Height: 2.39m
Weight: 11.590kg (laden)
10,500kg (unladen)
Engine: Rolls-Royce B80 Mk 6A 8-cylinder petrol
engine developing 180bhp at 3,750rpm
Crew: 3
No of Wheels: 6 × 6
Speed: 72kph
Range: 400km
Gradient: 42%
Fording Depth: 1.07m
Armament: 1 × 76mm gun and 43 rounds of
ammunition, 1 × 7.62mm MG coaxial with main
armament, 1 × 7.62mm MG for commander,
2 × 6-barrelled smoke dischargers

Development

The first prototype Saladin was completed in 1954
by Alvis of Coventry, and the production run was
ended in 1972. The vehicle deserves mention in this
volume due to its service in the IS role in many
armies. What is not so generally known is that the
German Frontier Police also have in service a
number of Mk 2 Saladins in the D version without
the coaxial MG and fitted with some German
equipment. The German designation is SW-111
KFz-93 Geschützer Sonderwagon III.

Employment

Abu Dhabi, Bahrain, Ceylon, German Border Police,
Ghana, Indonesia, Jordan, Kenya, Kuwait, Libya,
Muscat and Oman, Nigeria, Portugal, Qatar, South
Yemen, Sudan, Tunisia, Uganda and the United
Kingdom.

Right: *Alvis Saladin
armoured car.*

Alvis Saracen APC   UK

Right: *Alvis Saracen APC.*

Length: 5.233m
Width: 2.539m
Height: 2.463m
Wheeltrack: 2.08m
Wheelbase: 1.524m
Weight: 10.413kg (laden)
8,640kg (unladen)
Engine: Rolls-Royce B80 Mk 6A 8-cylinder petrol engine developing 170bhp at 3,750rpm
Crew: 12
No of Wheels: 6 × 6
Speed: 72kph
Range: 400km
Gradient: 42%
Vertical Obstacle: .46m
Fording Depth: 1.07m
Turning Radius: 13.72m
Max Side Slope: 45%
Armament: 1 × 7.62mm MG in turret, 1 × 7.62mm

MG on ring mount at rear of vehicle, 2 × 3 barrelled smoke dischargers

Development

The first Saracen prototype was built in 1952, and the production run was ended in 1972 at Alvis of Coventry. The Saracen has been used in the IS role in many parts of the world, and is still used widely by the British Army in Northern Ireland. Its armour varies between 8mm and 16mm in thickness.

Variants

FV 604 Command Post and FV 610 Command Post.

Employment

Abu Dhabi, Brunei, Hong Kong Police, Indonesia, Jordan, Kuwait, Libya, Nigeria, Qatar, South Africa, Sudan, Thailand, Uganda, United Kingdom.

Daimler Ferret Mk 5 Scout Car   UK

Length: 3.96m
Width: 2.13m
Height: 2.08m
Ground Clearance: .41m
Wheelbase: 2.286m
Wheeltrack: 1.75m
Weight: 5,890kg (laden)
4,980kg (unladen)
Engine: Rolls-Royce B60 Mk 6A 6-cylinder, water-cooled petrol engine developing 129bhp at 3,750rpm
Crew: 2
No of Wheels: 4 × 4
Speed: 80kph
Range: 300km
Gradient: 46%
Vertical Obstacle: .4m
Fording Depth: .9m

Development:

The first Mk 1 Ferret was completed by Daimler in 1949. Production of the Mk 5 continued until 1971. The Ferret was further developed into the Fox, which started production in 1973. The Ferret has been used in IS situations throughout the world, and is currently used by the British Army in Northern Ireland.

Variants

Ferret Mk 1/1 (Scout Car Liaison open topped version), Mk 1/2 (Scout Car Liaison with small turret), Mk 2/2 (two door MG turret), Mk 2/3 (Scout Car Reconnaissance with 7.62mm MG in a turret),

Above: *Ferret Mk 2 on patrol in Londonderry, Northern Ireland.*

Mk 2/6 (Scout Car Reconnaissance guided weapon), Mk 3 (modified Mk 1/1), Mk 4 (rebuilt Mk 2), Mk 5 (rebuilds of earlier vehicles).

Employment

Abu Dhabi, Bahrain, Brunei, Burma, Cameroon, Canada, Ceylon, France, Gambia, Ghana, Iran, Indonesia, Iraq, Jamaica, Jordan, Kenya, Kuwait, Libya, Malagasy, Malawi, Malaysia, Muscat and Oman, New Zealand, Nigeria, Qatar, Ras-Al-Khaimah, Rhodesia, Saudi Arabia, Sierra Leone, South Yemen, Sudan, Uganda, Upper Volta, Zaire, Zambia.

GKN Sankey AT-104 IS Vehicle   UK

Length: 5.49m
Width: 2.44m
Height: 2.49m (to standard cupola roof)
Ground Clearance: .51m
Wheeltrack: 1.72m
Wheelbase: 3.33m
Weight: 8.074kg (unladen)

Engine: A number of petrol or diesel power units can be fitted to provide a power range of 100 to 150bhp. The standard vehicle uses well proven units from General Motors
Crew: 11
No of Wheels: 4 × 4
Speed: 80kph

Range: 500km
Gradient: 50%
Fording Depth: 1m
Max Side Slope: 30%
Armament: In its standard form the AT-104 has no vehicle-mounted armament but the cupola can be replaced in manufacture with a specially designed turret to mount single or twin MGs of 7.62mm or 5.56mm calibre. Alternatively a MG can be externally mounted. Grenade launchers can also be fitted

Development/Variants

The AT-104 was developed from the 1-tonne 4 × 4 Humber Pig (FV 1611) armour truck, which is the Humber FV 1601 truck chassis powered by a 120hp 6-cylinder Rolls-Royce B-60 Mk 5A petrol engine on which was mounted an armoured shell produced by

GKN Sankey and the Royal Ordnance Factories. The AT-100 (4 × 2) and the AT-104 (4 × 4) were produced in 1972 by GKN Sankey to meet the specific requirements of anti-urban guerilla operations. Utilising Bedford civilian truck parts already in production in order to keep down costs, these vehicles are among the first to have been specially designed for this type of work. The AT-104 has a number of optional items which can be fitted on request. These include spotlights, a hydraulic winch, a loudspeaker system, a barricade remover, flashing bacons and/or sirens and several more.

Employment

Netherlands Police, Brunei Army. (Also some 500 uparmoured Humber Pigs are still in service with the British Army in Northern Ireland.)

GKN Sankey AT-105 IS Vehicle   UK

Right: *GKN Sankey AT-105 on trials.*

Length: 5.17m
Width: 2.49m
Height: 2.63m (to top of cupola)
Ground Clearance: .36m
Wheeltrack: 2.02m
Wheelbase: 3.07m
Weight: 8,340kg (unladen)
Engine: General Motors Bedford type 500 6-cylinder diesel developing 147hp at 2,800rpm *or* Rolls-Royce B81 8-cylinder developing 164hp at 3,000rpm
Crew: 10
No of Wheels: 4 × 4
Speed: 96kph
Range: 510km
Gradient: 70%
Vertical Obstacle: .41m
Fording Depth: 1.12m
Turning Radius: 8.84m
Max Side Slope: 36%
Armament: The standard AT-105 has an observation command cupola only (see photo) with or without a pintle mounted MG. Alternatively a single or twin 7.62mm GP MG turret can be fitted.

Smoke dischargers can be fitted to either.

Development

The new AT-105 developed by GKN Sankey of Telford, Shropshire, has been specifically designed for anti-riot requirements in urban areas, and for counter insurgency and guerilla warfare. As such, the standard vehicle has no fixed armament, though a turret is available if desired. The hull is resistant to 5.56mm and 7.62mm AP or ball at point-blank range. The specially shaped hull avoids mine blast pockets and affords maximum protection to the crew, engine, gearbox and radiator. The run-flat tyres are fitted as standard. Accessability is excellent due to two large doors in the rear, which are controlled by the driver, and two side doors. There are six observation/firing ports, and the driver has four small windows fitted with bullet-proof glass giving the same degree of protection as the armour plate. The same optional extra items are available as for the AT-104. Although neither sophisticated nor complex, since the designer's aims were simplicity and economy, this vehicle is in fact the world's first to be designed expressly to meet today's IS requirement. Other vehicles have IS variants or have been adapted for IS use. Production of the AT-105 started in 1977.

Variants

There are four variants other than the two IS variants discussed above. The first mounts a 20mm or 25mm cannon providing an anti-aircraft/helicopter

capability. There is also an 81mm mortar vehicle, a command post version, and lastly a fire support version mounting the 76mm Scorpion turret.

Employment

The AT-105 has aroused interest in many countries. The Malaysian Army is currently evaluating the vehicle.

Glover Armoured Car   UK

Length: 4.37m
Width: 1.65m
Height: 2.14m
Wheelbase: 2.77m
Weight: 2,285kg (unladen)
Engine: 6-cylinder petrol engine developing 86bhp
Crew: 9

Development

The Glover Armoured Car is manufactured by Glover, Webb & Liversidge Ltd. Designed to transport nine men including the driver and commander, the Glover is based on the Land Rover 2.77m wheelbase one ton military chassis. The sides, rear and front of the body are fabricated from 6.4mm special armoured steel plate, proof against 7.62mm and .30in ball ammunition at a range of approximately 10m and providing substantial protection against AP rounds. The roof and engine compartment are constructed from 4.7mm armoured steel plate, the double flap observation hatch in the roof being made of 6.4mm armoured steel. The floor can be armoured variously with 4.7mm aluminium or glass reinforced plastic supplied by Bristol Composites. Observation/gun

Above: *Glover armoured car.*

ports are provided in the sides and front and rear doors.

Employment

Thai Army.

Glover Armoured Land Rover   UK

Development

Glover, Webb & Liversidge have adapted a 2.77m wheelbase Land Rover to provide ballistic protection against 9mm ammunition. The vehicle has an armour plated floor for protection against mines. The vehicle is suitable for the transport of VIPs, the rear

compartment having leather seats and a glazed partition between the cab and the VIP compartment.

Employment

Details not available.

Left: *Glover armoured Land Rover.*

Glover Land Rover Escort Vehicle

UK

Development

Glover, Webb & Liversidge of Hamble have developed a 2.77m wheelbase Land Rover into an armoured escort vehicle able to withstand automatic weapons with a muzzle velocity of up to 1,000ft/sec. Suitable for a 4/6 man crew, and equipped with a roof hatch, gun ports and floor plates, the vehicle is intended for use as an escort vehicle by police.

Employment

Details not available.

Right: Glover Land Rover escort vehicle.

Glover Thracian Special Support Vehicle

UK

Length: 5.538m
Width: 2.22m
Height: 2.718m
Ground Clearance: .25m approx
Wheelbase: 2.439m (front)
1.194m (rear)
Weight: 8,860kg (less crew)
Engine: Mercedes-Benz 5,670cc turbo charged diesel driven 6-cylinder unit developing 168bhp
Crew: 9
No of Wheels: 6 × 4
Speed: 100kph approx
Range: 800km approx
Turning Radius: 10.5m

Development

Developed by Glover, Webb and Liversidge, the Thracian, termed a Special Support Vehicle, was first unveiled at the 1978 British Army Equipment Exhibition. It is at present in prototype form but negotiations are already underway with several customers. The vehicle is designed as a command vehicle for riot, hijack, kidnap or seige operations.

The Thracian is armoured to protect against 7.62mm NATO ball at point-blank range, and 5.56mm ball at 40m fired from rifles. Fuel tanks are also armoured and 'Explosafe'. Standard equipment includes: closed circuit television with pneumatic hoist, radio link television, time lapse video tape equipment, real time cassette video tape equipment, multi-channel sound tape recording equipment, high band VHF radio communications, low band VHF radio communications, UHF radio communications, telephone, independent power supply facilities, external power pick-up point, air conditioning and ventilation, lighting, heating, siren/public address system, fire extinguishers and portable bullet resistant shields.

Optional equipment includes: cryptographic voice security equipment, UHF hand-portable radios, audio surveillance equipment, radio link television remote control equipment, photographic surveillance equipment, night vision devices, closed circuit television image intensification camera, specialist search equipment, portable explosive detector, lightweight portable hydraulic jacks, tool kits, axes and crowbars, portable high powered searchlights, self-contained breathing apparatus, climbing and abseil equipment, comprehensive medical pack and stretcher, specialist clothing and bullet resistant helmets and jackets.

Employment

Negotiations are underway with several foreign armies.

Right: Glover Thracian.

Glover Tuareg Remote Area Patrol Vehicle

Length: 5.4m
Width: 2.28m
Height: 2.009m
Ground Clearance: .381m
Wheelbase: 2.8m
Weight: 5,860kg (less crew)
Engine: Mercedes-Benz 3-litre 6-cylinder petrol driven unit developing 156bhp
Crew: 3-5
No of Wheels: 4 x 4
Speed: 100kph approx
Range: 1,600-2,250km dependent upon terrain
Turning Radius: 13m
Armament: 2 x 7.62mm GPMG, 84mm medium anti-tank weapon, 4 x electrically-operated grenade dischargers

Development

The Glover, Webb and Liversidge Tuareg was unveiled at the 1978 British Army Equipment Exhibition. It is included in this volume because it is the first purpose built Remote Area Patrol Vehicle. Although it is only at present in its prototype form, negotiations are thought to be underway with one or more Middle East armies to purchase substantial numbers of this vehicle.

The Tuareg is a 4 x 4 long range patrol vehicle with aluminium body work and limited armoured protection in certain vital areas. The fuel tank has a capacity of 445 litres (100 UK gallons) in three tanks with armoured protection and fitted with 'Explosafe'. Additional general equipment includes 2 x 113 litre (25 UK gallons) water tanks, a winch with 2,728kg pull, two spare wheels, sand channels, night driving lamps, an 8in 100w searchlight, and a variety of other items.

Navigational equipment can include a theodolite and tripod, a sun compass, magnetic compass, and a Decca radio navigational receiver Mk 23. Communications equipment includes one UK VRC 353 VHF TX/RX, one UK VRC 321 HF TX/RX, one UK VRC 322 HF 250w amplifier, encryption equipment, a 13m telescopic antenna mast, and a portable 24v DC 1.5kw generator.

The Tuareg is designed for IS duties in remote areas, particularly desert, and it is of course ideal for covert operations.

Employment

The Tuareg is still in the development stage but, while it is not possible to publish details, this vehicle is likely to be in service with some Middle Eastern armies in the near future.

Below: *Glover Tuareg.*

GRP- and Macralon-Armoured Vehicles   UK

Left: *Bedford 4 ton truck covered with GRP armour.*

Development

The British Army have developed GRP and Macralon Armour for standard Land Rovers and Bedford 4-ton cargo trucks. GRP is a form of fibreglass and it gives some protection against low velocity SA fire, acid bombs, and Claymore fragments. GRP is used to cover the body and roof of vehicles, while Macralon, a form of strengthened plastic, is used to cover windscreens and windows.

Employment

British Army.

Hotspur Armoured Land Rover   UK

Above: *Hotspur armoured Land Rover.*

Length: 4.572m (overall)
Width: 1.676m (overall)
Height: 1.905m (overall)
Weight: 2.17kg (overall) 727kg (additional armour)
Speed: 100kph

Development

Trevor Davies have developed an 'add-on' armouring kit for Land Rover, Toyota Landcruiser and Willys Jeep vehicles, giving protection against multi-hits by 7.62mm ball rounds at 40m. The kit can be fitted in such a way that the normal appearance of the vehicle is virtually unaffected, and the same kit can be readily transferred to another similar vehicle in the event of mechanical breakdown. Included in the kit is a fully welded body unit complete with seats for six persons, fabricated of 4.76mm Hotspur steel, plus rear doors (also Hotspur steel) and windscreen, side and rear windows made of 29mm laminated armoured glass. The vehicle floor at front and rear is protected by GRP laminates. Air conditioning, heavy duty springs and shock absorbers are fitted as standard.

Variants

The Hotspur Armoured Land Rover APC is the same as the Armoured Land Rover, except that it is camouflaged, and is fitted with CS Gas dischargers, a spotlamp, a public address system, and a barricade remover. The overall length is increased by .762m and the overall height by .559m.

Employment

The Hotspur Armoured Land Rover is the basic patrol vehicle of the Royal Ulster Constabulary.

Hotspur Armoured Saloon Cars UK

Development

Hotspur have adapted the Rolls-Royce Silver Shadow as a DOV or VIP vehicle. Details of armouring are not available. However, the ballistic performance is high. Several of these vehicles have

been delivered to customers in the Middle East. The vehicle illustrated has been fully armoured.

Employment

Precise details not available.

Hotspur Mamba IS Vehicle UK

Development

Details of the Hotspur Mamba prototype are not available. However, the manufacturers state that the vehicle is intended for IS situations where an extremely fast and highly manoeuvrable vehicle is

required, possibly in a hijack situation. It has a top speed of over 90mph, and the armour is reported to be capable of stopping a NATO 7.62mm ball round.

Employment

Prototype available only.

Left: *Hotspur Mamba prototype.*

Mondart IS Vehicle UK

Length: 5.334m
Width: 1.778m
Height: 2.16m
Wheelbase: 2.54m + .902m
Weight: 4,100kg (unladen)
Engine: Rover V-8 petrol engine developing 130bhp

at 5,000rpm
Crew: 8
No of Wheels: 6 x 4
Speed: In excess of 120kph
Range: 500km approx
Turning Radius: 14m

Above: *Mondart IS vehicle.*

Development

Mondart IS vehicles are being designed, built and marketed by a consortium of three companies. Mondart Enterprises Ltd are responsible for design and marketing. Carmichael Fire and Brick Ltd are responsible for converting the Range Rover chassis to a 6 × 4 specification, and Trevor Davies & Sons Ltd are responsible for providing the armoured protection. The basis of the conversion is the 6 × 4 version of the Range Rover chassis. A special 4.76 or 6.35mm steel armour plate is used in all conversions to give a high protection to crew and engine compartments. Windows are fitted with a 29mm thick bullet resistant glass, and three gun ports per side and one in each rear door are provided. The very high gross power/weight ratio of 32bhp per ton gives excellent mobility. What makes this vehicle particularly suitable for some IS roles, such as airport security or covert surveillance, is the low profile of the vehicle. The vehicle will not excite the emotions of moderate majorities, nor will it be easily identified as a police or para-military vehicle. It is a classic DOV.

Variants

Armoured Ambulance, Mobile Operations Centre, Special Surveillance Vehicle, Airport Surveillance Vehicle.

Employment

Prototype only available.

Pyrene Water Cannon UK

Left: *Pyrene water cannon.*

Development/Variants

Designed for urban riot control purposes, the Pyrene Water Cannon Truck design can be adapted to fit any suitable vehicle, and is in this case fitted to a British Government supplied Foden 20/40ton 6 x 4 chassis. A clean body design inhibits unauthorised mounting of the vehicle, and prevents lodging of missiles, such as petrol bombs, on the structure. General construction is a welded steel framework panelled in mild steel sheets, the front of the crew compartment in 12 SWG, the remainder of the crew compartment in 14 SWG. Windscreens are in 11mm laminated glass and side windows in 5mm Macrolon. The cannon is controlled by an operator in an 11mm bullet resistant glass cupola above the crew compartment. Traverse is 180°+ and elevation and depression limits are 45° and 15° respectively.

The performance is infinitely variable according to a number of characteristics including pump and tank capacity, exemplified as follows:

Cannon nozzle size: 24mm
Water pressure: 54.4kg
Water throughput: 1,246 litres per min
Water tank capacity: 7,264 litres (fixed)
Duration (continuous): 5.5min approx
Effective jet length: 30m approx

Optional equipment includes a tank containing a liquid dye concentrate, connected through suitable valves and an inductor unit to introduce a dye into the water stream en route to the cannon. A searchlight can be mounted coaxially on the cannon, and screen wipers fitted to the cupola. The screen washers can be duplicated to spray both water and paint solvent.

Employment

British Army.

Shorland Mk 3 Armoured Car   UK

Length: 4.6m
Width: 1.78m
Height: 2.29m (to turret roof)
Wheeltrack: 1.36m
Wheelbase: 2.77m
Weight: 2,931kg (unladen), 3,360kg (laden)
Engine: Rover petrol 6-cylinder developing 91bhp at 4,500rpm
Crew: 3
No of Wheels: 4 x 4
Speed: 88kph
Range: 514km
Gradient: 60%
Fording Depth: 1m
Turning Radius: 17.75m
Armament: A variety of armament can be mounted in the turret, but experience has shown that preference is for the standard NATO 7.62mm GPMG

Development

The origins of the Shorland Mk 3 go back to the mid-1960s when the Royal Ulster Constabulary asked Shorts to study the question of producing a light armoured vehicle suitable for IS and border patrol work. To meet the request for maximum simplicity and lowest possible cost, the General Engineering Division of Short Brothers and Harland of Newtonards, Northern Ireland, converted the long wheel base version of the Land Rover by reinforcing the suspension and axles to take account of the weight of the armour, and by modifying the gear ratios. The Mk 1 produced 67hp at 4,100rpm, the Mk 2 77hp and the Mk 3 91hp at 4,500rpm. The armoured shell varies in thickness between 8.25 and 11mm and can withstand 7.62mm NATO ammunition at close range, while the Triplex windscreen can be rapidly covered with an armoured shield fitted with vision slots. A special material based on glass reinforced plastic is used in the floor of the vehicle, and has shown itself to afford good protection against mines. The turret is manually operated and rotatable through 360°. Searchlights and/or passive night vision equipment can be fitted.

Employment

Following its initial employment with the Royal Ulster Constabulary, the Mk 3 was issued to the British Army for use in Northern Ireland, and to date has been exported to 20 or so countries including Argentina, Brunei, Libya, many of the Persian Gulf States, Thailand and Venezuela.

Right: *Shorland Mk 3 armoured patrol car.*

Shorland SB-301 IS APC   UK

Length: 4.29m
Width: 1.77m
Height: 2.16m
Wheeltrack: 1.36m
Wheelbase: 2.77m
Weight: 3,545kg (laden)
Engine: Rover petrol 6-cylinder developing 91bhp at 4,500rpm
Crew: 8
No of Wheels: 4 × 4
Speed: 96kph
Range: 368km
Gradient: 50%
Fording Depth: 1m
Turning Radius: 17.75m

Development

The Shorland SB-301 was developed from the Shorland Mk 3 Armoured Car (see page 31). It was developed as a practical and cost effective solution to the safe transport of personnel under operational conditions in an IS situation. With the same engine and mechanics of the Mk 3, and therefore with a similar performance, the SB-301 can carry eight men, of which two travel in the front. Protection is similar to that of the Mk 3, and is effective against 7.62mm at short range. The roof is ridged to ensure that hand thrown missiles roll off when the vehicle is stationary.

Employment

Royal Ulster Constabulary, British Army, Netherlands Airport Police, and 20 vehicles have been ordered by two undisclosed countries.

Below: Shorland SB-301 IS APC.

Cadillac Gage Commando V-150 APC   USA

Length: 5.69m
Width: 2.26m
Height: 1.96m (to hull roof)
Ground Clearance: .38m
Wheeltrack: 2.1m
Wheelbase: 2.85m
Weight: 6,804kg (unladen) 9,185kg (laden)
Engine: Chrysler gasoline 361 210hp or Cummins diesel V6 155hp
Crew: 12
No of Wheels: 4 ×4
Speed: 90kph
Range: 750km
Gradient: 60%
Vertical Obstacle: 608m

Fording Depth: Swims
Turning Radius: 16.7m
Max Side Slope: 30%
Armament: Externally mounted MG or manual turret mounting twin .30cal twin 7.6mm/.30-.50cal combination MGs

Development

A prototype of the Commando was produced in March 1963 and it went into production in 1964. The Commando uses many components already in use in other vehicles, such as the Rockwell Standard axles used in the M-34 series of trucks and the 210hp Chrysler V-8 engine used in the M-113 APC. The Commando, which proved itself in Vietnam, has

Left: *Cadillac Gage Commando V-150.*

excellent mobility with a high top speed, a good range, and can carry 12 men. It offers good protection against inflammable liquids and close range small arms fire, and individual weapons can be fired through ports.

Variants

There are three different models of hull, (V-100, V-150 and V-200). The V-100 is the basic version, while the V-150 has stronger suspension and axles and can be fitted with a different engine and transmission. The V-200 is powered by a 275hp diesel. All versions are available in a wide range of

configurations, of which three are suitable for IS duties: the simple turretless APC, the turreted version and the fixed superstructure version which can be used as a mortar or command vehicle.

Employment

US Air Force (for airbase protection), US Army, various US Police forces, Turkish Police, Mexican Army and some 16 other armies or police forces, including those of Bolivia, Ethiopia, Laos, Lebanon, Muscat and Oman, Peru, Portugal, Saudi Arabia, Somalia, Sudan and Singapore.

BTR-152 APC USSR

Length: 6.553m
Width: 2.311m
Height: 2.007m
Ground Clearance: .305m
Weight: 8,950kg (laden)
Engine: ZIL-123 6-cylinder in line petrol engine developing 110bhp at 2,900rpm
Crew: 17
No of Wheels: 6
Range: 644km
Gradient: 55%
Vertical Obstacle: .6m
Fording Depth: .8m
Armament: 1 x 7.62mm SGMB MG

Development

The BTR-152 APC first appeared in 1950 and was based on the ZIL-151 truck chassis. Later models of

the BTR-152 used the ZIL-157 chassis. This vehicle is the most widely used of Soviet vehicles in IS situations.

Variants

BTR-152V (with variable tyre pressure system), BTR-152K (with overhead armour), BTR-152U (command vehicle) and the BTR-152V (with twin 14.5mm guns).

Employment

Afghanistan, Albania, Algeria, Cambodia, Ceylon, China, Congo, Cuba, East Germany, Egypt, Guinea, Hungary, India, Indonesia, Iran, Iraq, Israel, Mongolia, North Korea, North Yemen, Palestine Liberation Army, Poland, Rumania, Somalia, Soviet Union, Sudan, Syria, Tanzania, Uganda, Yugoslavia.

Left: *BTR-152 deployed in Prague and manned by Soviet military police.*

33

Section II: Anti-Riot Equipment

Anti-riot equipment includes tear (CS) gas grenades and launchers, PVC and rubber projectiles, tear gas generators, various aerosol CS gas dispensers, riot shotguns, sniper rifles, batons and shocksticks. Most of this equipment entails the wearing of gas masks, a selection of which are also included in this section.

In a riot situation it is usually preferable for troops or police to maintain a reasonable distance between themselves and the crowd. This is not always possible and, when close contact is unavoidable, the most common means of crowd control is the wooden baton. It is not intended to cover batons in this section; however a recent development of the baton is the shockstick, which gives an uncomfortable, though not dangerous, electric shock.

CS grenades can be thrown by hand, or fired from a variety of anti-riot weapons including shotguns, grenade launchers and conventional rifles. Many of these anti-riot weapons can also fire anti-riot batons of various sizes and materials. Both rubber and PVC projectiles are available, and are designed to counter petrol bombers or stone throwing crowds, and to cause no more than bruising or shock.

In some situations, for instance when snipers fire at troops or police, security forces may have no alternative but to use rifles. Conventional small arms are described in detail in *Infantry Weapons of the World* by Christopher Foss. However, in some circumstances, such as in a hijacking or kidnapping incident, it may be necessary to use highly accurate weapons to avoid injury to innocent hostages or bystanders. Some sniper rifles especially designed for this purpose are therefore included in this section.

No attempt has been made to provide comprehensive cover of all anti-riot equipment in service throughout the world. One gas mask or CS grenade looks much like another. Therefore a reasonable international cross section representing all the main categories of anti-riot equipment has been chosen.

FN Tear Gas Grenades (CS)   Belgium

GRENADE LAC M1

Weighing 230g, it can be launched by hand, by rifle, or even from certain machine pistols. Its maximum range is 100m. It is the only grenade that can be launched by a rifle, including the Riot Shotgun (see page 36), without using any special launcher. The dimensions of the percussion shaft and the type of grenade cartridge are varied according to the launcher.

GRENADE LAC M2

Weighing approximately 475g, it is designed to be fired from a rifle fitted with a grenade launcher. Its maximum range is 160m. The grenade cartridge is varied according to the weapon used.

GRENADE LAC M3

Weighing 450g, it is for throwing by hand only.

GRENADE LAC M4

Weighing 400g, this grenade can be thrown by hand or fired by a rifle or grenade launcher.

GRENADE LAC M5

Weighing 123g, this grenade ignites by striking the lighter on the top cover.

Below: *Riot scene in Northern Ireland.* / The Times

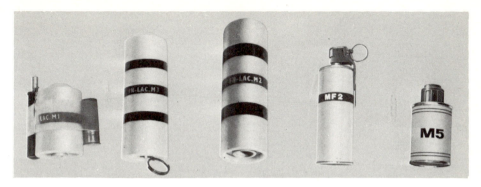

Development

FN (Fabrique Nationale) developed this family of CS tear gas grenades for use with police forces. The short time in which they ignite and the intensity of the cloud of gas make it virtually impossible for these grenades to be thrown back by demonstrators. In addition the grenades are made of plastic, and the danger of being burned by the melting plastic during the emission of gas is a further deterrent to the demonstrator.

Above: FN tear gas grenades.

Variants

In addition FN make two versions of tear gas grenades in metal containers.

Employment

Belgian and other police forces.

FN Tear Gas Aerosols (CN)   Belgium

AIDE MODEL

Scarcely larger than a pencil, and fitted with a stylo clip, it is hooked to the inside of a pocket. It disperses an efficient CN gas cloud at short range.

DEPUTY MODEL

Slightly larger than the 'Aide' model, the 'Deputy' provides an effective gas cloud against several individuals. Its capacity is about 70 jets of one second each.

Development

The tear gas aerosol, carried in a container fixed to a waist belt or hidden under a garment, is tending to increasingly replace the conventional truncheon, and

was designed for both use by police forces and individuals for self protection. The use of a tear gas aerosol allows the policeman to avoid any hand to hand struggle whilst ensuring a rapid though short disablement of his opponent.

Variants

FN produce variants which can send out an accurate jet to a distance of five metres, and which can be inserted in locks or underneath doors to dislodge individuals entrenched inside a building.

Employment

Details not available.

FN C607 Gas Mask   Belgium

Development

The C607 Gas Mask is manufactured for FN by Pirelli. It has been designed specifically for IS purposes: while giving good protection it provides a field of view of vision of 180°. The gas mask is fitted with an acoustic membrane to give a speech facility.

Employment

Details not available.

Left: FN C607 gas mask.

FN Fusil 'Police' Riot Shotgun
Belgium

Calibre: 12 bore
Length: 1m
Length of Barrel: 52cm
Weight: 2.95kg
Magazine Capacity: 6 cartridges + 1 in chamber

Development

This pump action riot shotgun was developed by FN specially for urban operations, and can hit a target of one square metre at a distance of 20m with a variety of 12 bore cartridges, in particular the 'Dispersante' cartidge for use in riot situations. The weapon is capable of firing the FN M1 tear gas grenade to a range of 100m, and is provided with an efficient anti-recoil pad and a luminescent foresight allowing easier aiming in the twilight or badly lit streets.

Employment

Details not available.

Below: *FN Fusil 'Police' riot shotgun.*

FN Sharpshooter's Rifle
Belgium

Calibre: 7.62mm
Length of Barrel: 61cm
Weight: 4.9kg (without sight)
Magazine Capacity: 4 rounds + 1 in chamber

Development

FN developed the Sharpshooter's Rifle for situations in which highly accurate fire is required. With its moderate weight and an adjustable telescopic sight, a good shot can hit a small target at 600m. The weapon has an adjustable sling and a variable butt length, and is normally fitted with the Zeiss Diavari D telescopic sight.

Employment

Details not available.

Below: *FN sharpshooter's rifle.*

Mask Protective No 2 Mk 2/2

Canada

Development
The Canadian designed mask No 2 Mk 2/2 is designed to provide protection from all known toxicological agents to the respiratory tract, face and eyes. The C-1 canister contains activated charcoal which absorbs toxic gases. The approximate weight of the complete mask is 540g.

Employment
Canadian Armed Forces.

Right: *Mask protective No 2 Mk 2/2.*

Alsatex Tear Gas Grenades

France

INSTANTANEOUS Mk F4 TEAR GAS (CB) GRENADES
There are three variants of the Mk F4, the first of which is designed to be thrown by hand (1 in photo); the second is for normal rifle projection out to about 100m (2 in photo) and the third is for long range rifle projection out to about 200m (3 in photo).

PERSISTENT EFFECT TEAR GAS GRENADES
Alsatex also manufacture two grenades which give off a persistent and invisible lachrymatory cloud of gas. The first (4 in photo) is thrown by hand and has a 2.5sec delay. The second (5 in photo) is designed for rifle projection out to about 100m and has a six seconds delay.

Employment
French Army, Gendarmerie and CRS.

Below: *Alsatex tear gas grenades.*

Alsatex Grenade Projector Armoured Cowling   France

Right: Alsatex grenade projector armoured cowling.

Armament: Cowling is fitted with a shortened MAS 36-51 rifle firing F4 Alsatex grenades
Firing Rate: 6 rounds per minute
Firing Angle: +25° to +55° (elevation), ± 50° (azimuth)
Total Weight: 75kg
Range: 200m

Development

The Grenade Projector Armoured Cowling was developed for the Berliet 'Gendarmerie' IS vehicle (see page 11), although it can be fitted to other IS vehicles. It allows troops to launch CS grenades from within an armoured vehicle by engaging a grenade launcher in the device. It consists of a mechanically welded armoured cowling which can be fixed to the Berliet 'Gendarmerie's' forward right hatch. Port holes can be fixed to the cowling if desired for observation and aiming purposes. The cowling and its mounting device are a watertight assembly.

Employment

French Gendarmerie.

CRS Riot Shield   France

Development

The Riot Shield developed for the CRS is a simple but rugged steel shield which also provides protection against low velocity SA fire. The vendor is the French Ministry of the Interior.

Employment

French CRS.

Kurt Matter Gas Mask   Germany

Development

This gas mask was developed by Kurt Matter GmbH in Germany for IS use. It provides a good field of vision and the microphone, built into the side of the gas mask with a plug-in connection to the amplifier unit, (left in photo) allows the wearer to communicate via the amplifier/loudspeaker without loss of speech volume or distortion and without any extraneous noise. If the microphone is not required a closure cap supplied with the mask can be used to seal off the microphone opening.

Employment

Details not available.

Right: Kurt Matter gas mask.

Mauser Grenade Launcher

Germany/France

Length: .98m (including launcher)
Weight: 3.5kg (excluding grenade)
Rifle Calibre: 7.62mm
Grenade Calibre: 57mm
Range: 100m

Development
The Mauser Grenade Launcher has been developed

by Mauser for use by the CRS. It is designed to fire persistent and non-persistent CS gas grenades to a range of approximately 100m.

Employment
French CRS.

Mauser SP66 Sniper's Rifle

Germany

Calibre: 7.62mm
Length of Barrel: 68cm

Development
Designed specifically to aid law enforcement agencies in sniper/counter-sniper situations, the Mauser SP66 Rifle is particularly suitable for this type of role. The weapon is equipped with a muzzle brake and flash hider, and various telescopic sight mountings are available (standard is the Zeiss Davari Z with a variable magnification of ×1.5-6). Each

Above: Mauser SP66 sniper's rifle fitted with Zeiss Davari Z telescopic sight.

SP66 is fitted with a movable spring loaded cheek piece and an adjustable recoil pad. Passive or infra-red night vision devices can be fitted for use during the hours of darkness in lieu of telescopic sights.

Employment
Federal German Frontier Police GSG-9.

CBR No 15 A1 Gas Mask

Israel

Development
This Israeli gas mask has been developed by Shalon Chemical Industries Ltd, of Tel Aviv. Its highly efficient voice emitter, permitting the use of any radio equipment including loudhailers, makes it particularly suitable for use IS situations.

Employment
Israeli Armed Forces.

Right: CBR No 15 A1 gas mask showing speech facility.

Protectojet CS Fog Projector Israel

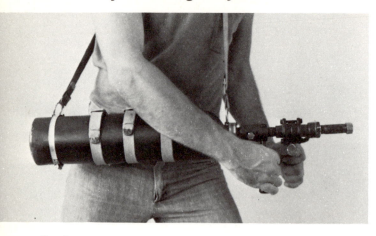

Left: Ispra Protectojet CS fog projector.

Development

This tear gas generator was developed in Israel by the Ispra-Israel Product Research Co Ltd, as an anti-terrorist weapon for use against groups of violent agitators in narrow streets and alleys. It is a highly effective method of CS gas dispensation. It has a range of 15m in still air, and will neutralise in five seconds any person within three metres either side of the line of fire. It weighs less than 9kg and is rechargeable.

Employment

Believed to be in use with Israeli Armed Forces.

Avery Discharger 1.5in and Launcher CS Grenade UK

Development

Both the Discharger 1.5in and Launcher CS Grenade can be fixed to the shortened version of the .303 No 4 Rifle with jungle butt. The 1.5in Discharger fires similar ammunition to the Avery AV Riot Gun, and is an ideal weapon for crowd disperal. The Launcher CS Grenade has a similar performance. A 7.62mm barrel can be fitted if required, and blank ammunition can be used for short ranges. A maximum range of 300m can be achieved by both equipments by using a stronger propellant. Normal range is about 150m. The equipment has been developed by W. A. Avery of London.

Employment

This equipment is not yet in production, but has been included as it is a cheap and practical solution to the crowd control problem.

Below: Rifle No 4 .303in; discharger 1.5in

Avery AV Riot Gun/Grenade Launcher

Above: *AV riot control gun/grenade launcher.*

Length: 83cm
Weight: 5.2kg
Effective Range: 65m
Max Range: 300m (high elevation)

Development

W. S. Avery & Sons conceived this riot gun. Currently under development the AV gun differs from previous designs in that it is a semi-automatic, magazine fed weapon operating on the blow-back principle. Initially configured to use all types of 1.5in riot control ammunition, the gun can readily be modified to fire 40mm HE grenades, so its use need not necessarily be limited to riot control situations. A four-round magazine is normally employed, but a larger magazine could also be fitted, this being attached on the right side of the gun and empty cases being ejected to the left. The fore hold on the barrel can be used as a pintle for armoured vehicles. An adjustable buffer is fitted in the butt tube to allow for differing propellents.

Employment

Not yet in production.

Lawrence, Scott and Electromotors Ltd Fire Discipline Range

Development

The Lawrence Scott & Electromotors Ltd of Norwich Fire Discipline Range has been developed to allow IS forces in training to discriminate between bona fide terrorist targets and innocent bystanders in an urban setting. It consists of a 'film set' type street scene with electrically driven dummy targets appearing in windows and around corners. Some are terrorists, some are not. The Fire Discipline Range is a valuable training aid.

Employment

British Army .

MOD Anti-Riot Equipment

Left: *EARP baton round projector.*

41

Right: *Lazy Tongs vehicle trap.*

Below right: *MBSD smoke discharger.*

EARP BATON ROUND PROJECTOR

EARP (Equipment Anti-Riot Projector) is used by the British forces to provide barrage fire capability for 1.5in baton rounds in riot situations. Mounted in an APC, EARP consists of four pintle-mounted barrels, each of which is mated to a 1.5in signal pistol. The vendor is the UK Ministry of Defence, (Sales).

Employment
British Army.

LAZY TONGS VEHICLE TRAP
Weight: 27.2kg (in box)
Length: 6.25m

Development
Developed for the British Army, Lazy Tongs is similar in function to existing spiked-chain-type vehicle traps but is more effective, and easier to transport by virtue of its concertina construction which enables it to be carried in a case. The 'tongs' can be rapidly pulled across a road in front of suspicious vehicles at check points etc, and will effectively immobilise most wheeled transport by puncturing their tyres. The light alloy spikes are readily replaceable if broken. A lightweight version (½ Lazy Tongs) is available for use by foot patrols. The vendor is the UK Ministry of Defence (Sales).

Variants
½ Lazy Tongs, weight 3.2kg, length 2m.

Employment
British Army.

MBSD SMOKE DISCHARGER
The Multi-Barrel Smoke Discharger (MBSD) is a fixed four-barrel vehicle-mounted equipment used to fire the L11 A1 Bursting CS discharger and the L5 A1 smoke discharger. The co-alignment and close grouping of the barrels permit the laying down of a rapid and dense CS barrage. The vendor is the UK Ministry of Defence (Sales).

Employment
British Army.

RSAF Grenade Launcher

UK

Below: *RSAF grenade launcher.*

Overall Length: 69.5cm
Weight of Launcher: 2.7kg
Weight of Grenade: 550g
Max Range: 100m

Development

Designed specifically as a portable launcher for the British LII Bursting CS Grenade, the Royal Small Arms Factory (Enfield) weapon is light and easy to handle. Power is provided by two standard size torch batteries, and a large number of grenades can be fired before replacement is necessary. The CS bursting grenade distributes approximately 23 smoke pellets over an area of approximately 25m diameter just before impact with the ground, providing a number of gas sources rather than a single plume.

Employment:

British Army .

SAS Developments SA121 Shockstick   UK

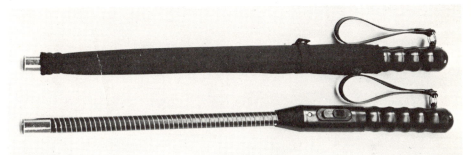

Length: 57.8cm
Weight: .54kg (including batteries)

Above: *SAS Developments SA121 shockstick.*

Development

The Shockstick, or protective staff, resembles a rolled umbrella in appearance. There, however, the resemblance ends. When switched on it emits a powerful charge of about 6,000-7,000v. However, it does not burn, or cause an injury. This is due to the very low milli-amp rating (a maximum of 8.3mA) and a wiring system which localises the shock, ie the recipient does not get a through body current and the shock is entirely confined to the small surface area which makes actual contact with the stick. It is designed to emit a loud crackling noise accompanied by blue static sparks flashing up and down the spiral element. This warns an assailant that he is confronted by something less innocuous than it appears. If he ignores this warning and grasps the stick, or is touched by it, he will be instantly repelled by an electric shock, but without suffering any harm or damage. The Shockstick is supplied by SAS Developments Ltd.

Employment

Details not available.

Schermuly 1.5in Anti-Riot Gun and Signal Pistol   UK

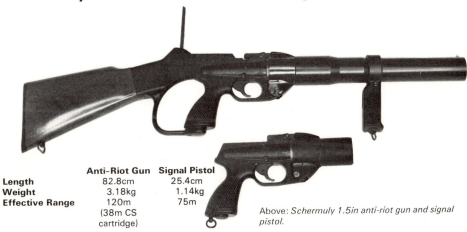

	Anti-Riot Gun	Signal Pistol
Length	82.8cm	25.4cm
Weight	3.18kg	1.14kg
Effective Range	120m	75m
	(38m CS cartridge)	

Above: *Schermuly 1.5in anti-riot gun and signal pistol.*

Development

This Webley-Schermuly lightweight smooth bore gun is a purpose-designed high quality weapon incorporating experience and techniques gained in service. It is constructed to give optimum performance with the variety of 38mm anti-riot cartridges and rounds now in service with, or under development for, the British Army. These include baton rounds and irritant cartridges. A major advantage of this gun in that the barrel is chambered to improve muzzle velocity and to give greater accuracy compared with other unchambered guns. It is built principally of high tensile aluminium alloy giving excellent durability and is a highly developed conventional single-shot, break-open weapon. The firing mechanism is of the double action type requiring a firm long trigger pull, and the striker has an automatic rebound to avoid accidental discharge when it is closing. The design also incorporates a safety interlock to ensure that the muzzle catch is full engaged before the weapon can be fired. Although principally used as a shoulder fired weapon, the gun can be used from a fixed mounting on armoured vehicles. The Signal Pistol uses the same basic components as the gun, but with the exclusion of the butt, and use of a shorter barrel. The pistol, though primarily used to fire smoke cartridges and signal flares, can also be used to fire baton rounds at closer ranges than the gun.

Employment

British Army, Royal Ulster Constabulary.

Schermuly 1.5in Anti-Riot Baton Round UK

Length of Round, complete: 12cm
Length of Projectile: 10.1cm
Diameter of Projectile: 3.7cm
Weight of Projectile: 135g
Weight of Round, complete: 170g
Muzzle Velocity: 100m/sec
Range: 60m

Development

The round was developed to deter individual petrol bombers or stone-throwing rioters at ranges of up to 60m. When used at the recommended ranges from a chambered weapon such as the Webley-Schermuly Anti-Riot Gun, a direct shot and not a ricochet is recommended to ensure selectivity and accuracy. Severe shock and bruising are then the maximum injuries likely to be sustained.

The 38mm Anti-Riot Rubber Baton Round has been designed as a cheaper alternative to the L3A1/L5A2 Plastic Baton Rounds supplied to the British MOD. The rubber round (bullet) equates in performance with the plastic rounds, and although designed specifically for use with the Webley-Schermuly multi-purpose gun, it can be fired from any 38mm riot gun or pistol. The round consists of a hardened rubber cylindrical projectile sealed in an aluminium cartridge case to make it waterproof.

Employment

British Army, Royal Ulster Constabulary.

Schermuly L3A1 1.5in Anti-Riot Irritant Cartridge UK

Length: 12cm
Weight: 200g
Range: 100m
Delay Time: 1.5sec
Burning Time: 10-25sec
Muzzle Velocity: 100m/sec

Development

The L3A1 irritant round carries a payload of CS smoke-producing composition, and can be fired from standard 1.5in pistols and riot guns. An aluminium canister projectile holds the CS smoke-producing composition and delay unit. This canister is contained within an aluminium cartridge case, which incorporates the percussion cap in the base and a propellant charge. For shorter ranges, an alternative round, having a reduced propellant charge, is available. When fired a delay composition is ignited by the propellant and emission of CS smoke begins a few seconds after firing.

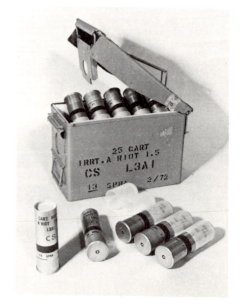

Right: *Schermuly 1.5in anti-riot irritant cartridge.*

Variants

A 'confusion round' of a rather different nature, being akin to a long-range thunderflash, is also available. This 75m-range, non-fragmenting round is used to produce a brilliant flash and report in the centre of a crowd, leading to its dispersal.

Employment

British Army, Royal Ulster Constabulary (L3A1 irritant round only).

Schermuly CS Grenades

UK

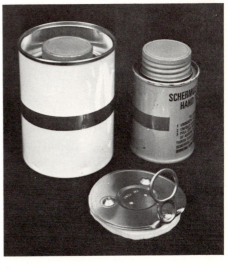

MODEL L1A3

Overall Length: 14cm
Overall Diameter: 6.4cm
Overall Weight: 454kg
Effective Range: Up to 30m
Burning Time: 10-40sec
Delay: 1-5sec

Development

The L1A3 was developed by Schermuly to provide a dense cloud of CS smoke for crowd control and dispersal. The grenade has a reinforced base plate enabling it to be launched from suitable rifle and AFV dischargers if required.

Employment

British Army.

MINI CS GRENADE

Overall Length: 9.2cm
Overall Diameter: 5.4cm
Overall Weight: 185kg
Effective Range: 50-60m
Burning Time: 5-15sec
Delay: 1.5-3sec

Development

The compact weight and size of the mini grenade give it several advantages over the L1A3 Grenade. The top cap of the grenade is unscrewed to expose the ignition ring, which in unfolded and pulled vertically away from the grenade body thus cocking and firing the grenade in one movement. The

Above: Schermuly CS mini grenade.

grenade is thrown immediately and in 1.5-3 seconds a plug is ejected and CS smoke is emitted.

Employment

Details not available.

Schermuly S/61 Lightweight Respirator

UK

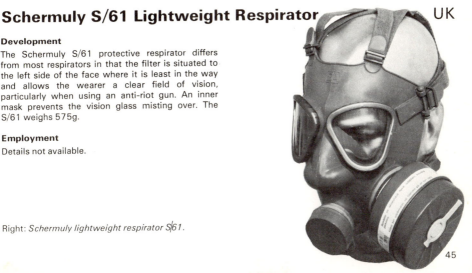

Development

The Schermuly S/61 protective respirator differs from most respirators in that the filter is situated to the left side of the face where it is least in the way and allows the wearer a clear field of vision, particularly when using an anti-riot gun. An inner mask prevents the vision glass misting over. The S/61 weighs 575g.

Employment

Details not available.

Right: Schermuly lightweight respirator S/61.

Schermuly SPAD

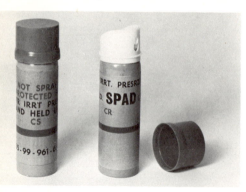

Above: *Schermuly SPAD.*

Length: 11.4cm
Diameter: 3cm
Weight: 93.39g
Effective Range: 4m

Development

Currently CR in a water based solution is the active element in the Self Protection Aid Device (SPAD) hand-held aerosol manufactured by Schermuly and supplied to British armed services. The chemical may also be supplied in prepacked and measured quantities for use with water-cannon equipment to dispel riot crowds. CR in this form is not a gas but a chemical additive. Therefore there is no possibility of contamination of neighbouring buildings if it is used in urban areas.

Employment

British Army.

Tannoy ALS25 Waist Hailer

UK

Development

The ALS25 has been designed for use by personnel wearing respirators, and is particularly useful for command and control during riots when CS smoke etc may have to be released. It consists of two parts, a loudspeaker with self-contained batteries (weight 1.8kg) which can be clipped to a web belt, and a microphone which can be stowed inside the loudspeaker assembly. The microphone clips on to the respirator on a swivel mounting which doubles as an on/off switch. When the wearer is using a radio or telephone handset the microphone can be pivoted out of the way. Using the ALS25 clear speech can be transmitted up to 180m.

Employment

British Army.

Webley Greener GP Mk II Riot Shotgun

UK

Above: *Webley Greener GP Mk II riot shotgun.*

Weight:
2.95kg with 71cm barrel
3.00kg with 76cm barrel
3.06kg with 81cm barrel
3.12kg with 86cm barrel
Overall Length:
113cm with 71cm barrel
118cm with 76cm barrel
123cm with 81cm barrel
128cm with 86cm barrel
Calibre: 12 bore only

Development

The Greener GP 12 bore was designed at the turn of the century by W. W. Greener, and is a development from the Martini-Henry rifle. Its design has remained essentially unchanged since. In use, an underlever lowers the falling block, ejects the spent cartridge, allows a new cartridge to be pushed home, cocks the gun and puts the safety catch on — all in one action. It is a conventional shotgun that has been used by police throughout the world, mostly in the British Commonwealth, for some 30 years.

Employment

British Army, South African Police, Egyptian Police, Malaysian Police, Kenyan Police, Cyprus Police, and other Commonwealth Police forces.

Mossberg Police/Military Riot Shotguns   USA

Development

Mossberg & Sons of North Haven, Connecticut, have developed a line of 12 bore riot guns for law enforcement. The guns are based upon the Model 500 system, except that guns are now available in either six or eight shot capacity. The Model 500 ATP8SP was introduced in January 1976. Barrel lengths are either 20in or 18½in and either standard bead sights or rifle sights can be supplied. A bayonet lug is supplied to allow the US M-7 Bayonet to be fitted if required.

Above: Mossberg 500 ATP6 18.5in barrel.

Variants

500 ATP6: 6 Shot, 18½in barrel, Bead sight (see photo); 500 ATP6S: 6 Shot, 18½in barrel, Rifle sight; 500 ATP8: 8 Shot, 20in barrel, Bead sight; 500 ATP8S: 8 Shot, 20in barrel, Rifle sight.

Employment

Various US Police Forces.

M33A1 Riot Control Agent Disperser   USA

Development

The M33A1 Riot Control Agent Disperser was developed in late 1974 by Tecom Engineering. It is used for control of riots in outdoor areas. Its payload of 11.4 litres (3gal) of 0.1% CR in a mixture of propylene glycol and water is dispersed through the gun nozzle by a compressed air supply. A four port rotatable nozzle on the end of the gun provides both spray and stream liquid agent capabilities up to 20m range with a discharge time of 25 seconds in either continuous or intermittent bursts. The disperser can be readily converted to dry powder riot control agent use by substituting the four port rotatable nozzle with a single port nozzle and replacing the agent container check valve assembly with an agitator assembly. 3-4kg of CS can be dispersed up to 15m range with a discharge time of 60-120 seconds in either continuous or intermittent bursts. Modular construction permits rapid turn around using pre-filled agent and air containers.

Employment

Details not available.

Remington Model 870P Police Gun   USA

Right: Remington Model 870P police gun.

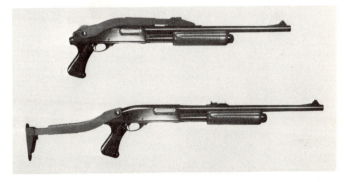

Weight: 3.4kg (with 50.8cm barrel)
Overall Length (butt extended):
102cm with 50.8cm barrel
97cm with 45.8cm barrel

Overall Length (butt folded):
77cm with 50.8cm barrel
72cm with 45.8cm barrel
Calibre: 12 bore only

47

Development

A new folding stock has been developed by Remington of Bridgeport, Connecticut, for the Remington Model 870P to meet the need for better close quarter handling characteristics and ease in carrying. The stock is held in the folded or extended position by an operating button, which, when depressed, swings the stock to the desired position. Conventional or plastic ammunition can be used. The plastic ammunition designated Modipac, is designed as a deterrent for use at ranges of 3-15m. At ranges of 20-25m the lightweight polyethylene pellets are not able to penetrate a sheet of newspaper. However at 3-15m the ammunition has an impressive deterrent effect. Since the shells are intended as a deterrent only, they are designed for use below knee level, and can even be bounced off the ground. Plastic pellets could cause eye injuries if the weapon is fired horizontally.

Variants

The Model 870 has a conventional stock.

Employment

Police Departments throughout the US, British Army.

Sherwood M-17 Gas Mask   USA

Development

Including the filter, the M-17 gas mask weighs only 0.91kg. It provides good protection against CN, CS and DM riot control gases.

Employment

US and Canadian Armed Forces, Singapore, Sudan, Thailand.

Soft/Sting Ring Airfoil Grenades   USA

Development

Soft and Sting type ring airfoil grenades (RAG) have been developed by Edgewood Arsenal's weapons systems concepts office at Aberdeen Proving Ground for Army military police as a means of controlling civil disturbances without close-up confrontation. The two RAG projectiles are fired from a launcher attached to a standard M-16 rifle used by the Army and National Guard as well as by numerous state and municipal police departments. The projectile configurations develop from a thick one-piece body of soft rubber material, shaped like an aerofoil and rolled into a ring. Both Soft and Sting projectiles have been developed to hit an individual at ranges varying from point-blank to approximately 50m, or to hit small groups at twice that distance, producing pain but a low probability of causing serious injury. Both projectiles, having the same weights and dimensions, are launched spinning at 5,000rpm providing gyroscopic stability during flight. A relatively flat flight brought about by this 'line of sight' path enables the user to aim directly and expect to hit the target. In addition the low drag shaping of the projectile allows it to retain a major portion of its kinetic energy during flight, thus remaining effective at long ranges. The Soft RAG is identical to Sting, except that it contains a small quantity of CS powder.

Above: *Ring airfoil grenade.*

Employment

US Army, US National Guard.

Smith & Wesson Grenades   USA

	Cont discharge No 2	Cont discharge No 3	Blast dispersion No 5	Rubber Ball No 15	Mighty Midget No 98
Overall Length:	15.2cm	14.5cm	15.2cm	11.8cm	12.7cm
Overall Diameter:	64mm	60mm	64mm	84mm	36mm
Effective Range:	30m	30m	30m	30m	50m
Burning Time (secs):	40/50	35/45	Inst	15/20	20/25
Delay (secs):	1-2	1-2	3	1-2	3

Development

Smith & Wesson have developed a comprehensive range of grenades using both CN or CS. In particular the Rubber Ball Grenade is worthy of special mention. This innovative grenade virtually eliminates the possibility of throwback and minimises the chance of injury.

Above left: Smith & Wesson continuous discharge grenades Nos 2 and 3.

Above: Smith & Wesson rubber ball No 15 grenade.

Employment

Various US police forces.

Smith & Wesson Chemical Mace Non-Lethal Weapons

USA

	Mk V	Mk III	Mk IX	Mk III Professional	Mk IV
Length:	16.5cm	10.1cm	1.9cm	11.8cm	15.8cm
Diameter:	37mm	23mm	58mm	25mm	37mm
Range (still air):	5m	3-4m	8m	3-4m	5m
Contents (1sec bursts):	35	20	60	30	40
Formulation:	CN	CN	CN	CN	CN
Gross Weight:	242g	40g	300g	59g	147g

Right: Smith & Wesson chemical Mace non-lethal weapons: from left to right, Mk V, Mk III, Mk IX, Mk III Professional, and Mk IV.

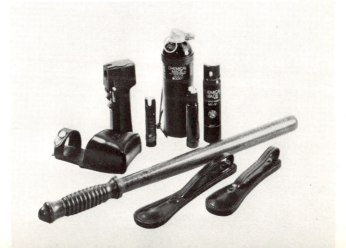

Development

In 1965 Chemical Mace Non-lethal Weapons were made available to police forces in the US by Smith & Wesson. Now, over 400,000 Chemical Mace Non-lethal Weapons are in service with 4,000 police departments in the US. All makes of the Smith & Wesson Non-lethal Chemical Mace Weapons are easily reloaded with a spare cartridge.

Employment

Various US police forces.

Smith & Wesson Riot Kits

USA

SHOTGUN TEAR GAS KIT

The addition of a chemical munitions capability makes the 12 bore shotgun a highly effective non-lethal weapons system. This Smith & Wesson shotgun Tear Gas kit contains a variety of CS or CN

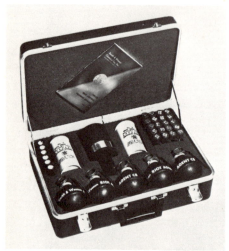

Tear Gas grenades, a 12 bore grenade launcher, and 20 Tru-flite Barricade projectiles.

MIGHTY MIDGET GRENADE KIT

This is a lightweight composite kit which contains 12 Mighty Midget grenades, either CS or CN, 12 Mighty Midget .38 special launching cartridges and a universal revolver launcher to fit any .38 Special or .357 Magnum revolver. The kit, which measures 19.2cm x 29.2cm x 9cm, weighs just 2.27kg.

PORTABLE RIOT CONTROL EMERGENCY KIT

This kit weighs 13.61kg, is 84.2cm long, 35.5cm wide, and 14cm deep. The kit contains a Smith & Wesson 37mm gas gun, 4 Tru-flite 37mm penetrating projectiles, 6 long-range 37mm projectiles, 6 short range 37mm shells and 4 continuous discharge grenades. All grenades and projectiles are available in CN or CS.

RIOT TRAINING KIT

This kit is housed in the same container as the Portable Riot Control Emergency Kit, but does not contain a 37mm gas gun. Instead it contains practice continuous discharge grenades, live smoke grenades, practice 37mm long range projectiles, a Chemical Mace aerosol, and two Chemical 'Wand' CS Disseminators. There are also CS and CN

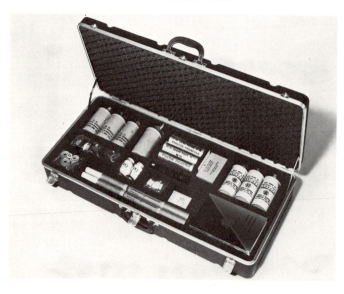

Above left: *Smith & Wesson shotgun tear gas kit.*

Left: *Smith & Wesson anti-riot training kit.*

50

capsules for training purposes, and spare grenade pins so that the practice continuous discharge grenades can be reused. In all this kit makes an extremely useful aid for training police forces in anti-riot techniques.

Employment

All these kits are in use with various US police forces, and are thought to have been purchased by some police forces in South America and the Far East.

Smith & Wesson Gasguns, Grenade Launchers and Launching Cartridges

USA

37mm GAS AND FLARE PISTOL

This pistol is designed to fire all Smith & Wesson 37mm projectiles (except for Tru-flite penetrating projectiles).

37mm SHOULDER GAS GUN

This gun will fire all 37mm projectiles. The barrel is detachable, the weight is under 2.7kg and the length is 73.7cm.

12 BORE LAUNCHER FOR CONTINUOUS DISCHARGE GRENADES

This heavy duty launcher is designed for use on Smith & Wesson and other 12 bore police shotguns for launching continuous discharge grenades (not illustrated).

12 BORE LAUNCHER FOR RUBBER BALL GRENADES

This launcher has been specifically designed to launch Smith & Wesson Rubber Ball grenades, and fits 12 bore shotguns (not illustrated). Other launchers are the 12 Bore Launching Cartridges for

Mighty Midget Grenades; .38 Special Mighty Midget Grenade Launcher.

Employment

Various US police forces, Indian Police.

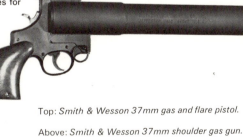

Top: *Smith & Wesson 37mm gas and flare pistol.*

Above: *Smith & Wesson 37mm shoulder gas gun.*

Smith & Wesson Pepper Fog Tear Smoke Generator

USA

Development

This tear smoke generator provides the effective output of thousands of cubic feet of CS and CN wherever it is required. Powered by a pulse jet engine the unit weighs less than 8.17kg and has the

fuel capacity for 45 minutes of continuous operation.

Employment

Various US police forces.

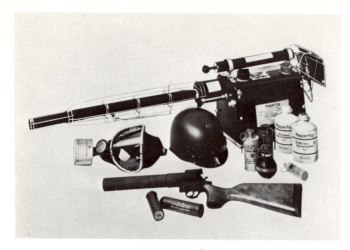

Left: *Smith & Wesson Pepper Fog tear smoke generator (also illustrated: Smith & Wesson gas mask, police helmet, 37mm gas gun and projectiles, and various gas grenades).*

Smith & Wesson Projectiles and Shells   USA

	Tru-Flite 37mm Projectile No 12	Long Range 37mm Projectile No 17	37mm Rubber Projectile No 18	Short Range 37mm No 21	Tru-Flite 12 bore Projectile No 23
Overall Length:	22cm	14cm	16.8cm	24.5cm	6.5cm
Overall Diameter:	37mm	37mm	37mm	37mm	12 bore
Effective Range:	100m	150m	150m	10m	80m
Burning Time (sec):	15-20	25-30	20-25	Instantaneous	Instantaneous
Delay (sec):	2	3	3	None	None

Development

Smith & Wesson Projectiles and Shells are designed to provide a stand off capability. The 12 bore projectile will penetrate and disseminate agent vapour behind 20mm plywood at 15m or window glass at 80m. All projectiles are available with either CS or CN smoke.

Employment

Various Police forces in US, Indian Police.

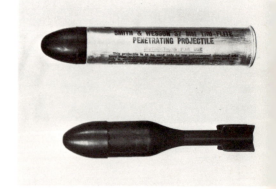

Right: *Smith & Wesson 37mm projectile.*

Smith & Wesson Gas Mask   USA

Development

Developed specifically for anti-riot situations, the Smith & Wesson Gas Mask is a lightweight and rugged item of equipment used widely throughout the United States.

Employment

Various US police forces.

Section III: Body Armour and Shields

Body armour is normally designed to protect only the most vulnerable parts of the body, namely the chest and the back. It is not feasible to provide full armoured protection for the head, except in the special case of bomb disposal, in which case every attempt is made to provide maximum protection for all parts of the body. This is at the expense of mobility and vision. Body armour therefore varies from the lightweight concealable undervests designed to provide protection against low velocity ammunition, to the heavier and more cumbersome EOD suits designed for bomb disposal. This section will also include protective headgear designed specifically for IS situations.

There are basically two types of shield, the one which is designed to be used in a riot situation and which can cope with stones, bricks and bottles, and the other which is proof against bullets. Helmets can also be fitted with special visors to protect the eyes against stones and the like. Riot shields and visors are constructed of a polycarbonate which is both shatterproof and fire resistant.

In addition this section will cover other forms of protection for IS personnel such as special armoured seats for helicopters, and special shatterproof films for large glass areas to counter bomb damage. Body armour, EOD suits, shields, special helmets, seat armour and visors now form a vital part of the equipment catalogue of an effective IS force. This section aims to cover the more important developments in this field.

FN Bullet-Proof Vests

Belgium

P100

Weight: with 2mm thick armour plate: 4.2kg
with 2.5mm thick armour plate: 5.1kg
with 3mm thick armour plate: 6kg

P200

Weight: with 2mm thick armour plate: 6.5kg
with 3mm thick armour plate: 10kg

Development

FN favour a type of bullet-proof vest made with synthetic material and fitted with steel plates, which suffer only a slight deformation at the moment of impact.

Variants

P400 (see photo). No specification available.

Employment

Belgian and other police forces.

Right: *FN P400 bullet-proof vest.*

FN Casemates

Belgium

Development

FN have developed the P700 (thickness 6.5mm, weight 370kg) and P800 (thickness 6.5mm, weight 590kg) Casemates for use in hijack or shoot-out situations. Both versions offer complete protection against NATO 7.62mm rounds. They are towable and have axle brakes though in operation they are manoeuvrable by the man or men they are protecting. They can, of course, also be used to approach an IED in order to inspect it.

Employment

Belgian police.

Right: *FN P800 casemate.*

FN Cromwell Helmet

Belgium

Development

The FN Cromwell Helmet is constructed of reinforced polyester fully lined with aired foam and set in a shock-proof rim. The helmet has an adjustable chin piece and a visor made from shock-proof plexiglass 5mm thick. The FN gas mask can be worn with the helmet.

Employment

Belgian Police.

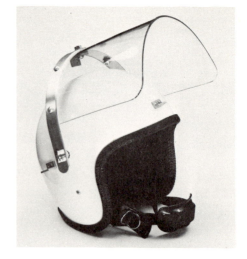

Right: *FN Cromwell helmet.*

FN Riot Shields

Belgium

SHIELD B10

The weight of the FN B10 Riot Shield is 3.2kg. It is proof against all types of missiles likely to be encountered in a riot situation. The circular variant is slightly lighter.

Employment

Belgian police.

Right: *FN riot shield.*

FN Bullet Resistant Shields

Belgium

SHIELD P400
Height: 60cm
Width: 50cm
Thickness: 2.5mm
Weight: 8kg

SHIELD B500
Thickness: 2mm (weight: 7kg) *or*
3mm (weight: 10.3kg)

Development
The B500 and P400 shields developed by FN are designed to withstand a strike by a 7.62mm round. The B500 is curved and can also be used for long periods by deploying the legs on the bottom of the shield. The P400 is a more conventional shield of flat, square design. Both shields are designed for use in shoot-out situations as protection against SA fire rather than in riot situations, for which they would be too heavy.

Employment
Belgian police.

Right: FN B500 shield.

Glaverbel VHR Glass

Belgium

Development
Laminated High Resistance Glass, as developed by Glaverbel-Mécaniver of Brussels, consists of two or more sheets of drawn or float glass. This combination offers a high mechanical and thermo-mechanical resistance, and is assembled with an interlayer of plastic known as polyvinyl butyval. The thickness of the glass must be appropriate to the type of arms and calibres against which protection is required, and to the number of shots the glass is expected to have to withstand. Providing the appropriate thickness of glass is provided, tests have shown that VHR glass can prevent penetration of bullets. For instance tests with VHR glass in Sweden in 1975 showed that one 7.62mm round from an AK4 rifle fired from five metres at 35mm thickness VHR glass did not achieve penetration, though there was a degree of spalling. Lower velocity weapons achieved no penetration and caused no spalling.

Employment
Glaverbel VHR Glass is used in various high risk buildings in Holland, Switzerland, Sweden and Belgium, and also by police on armoured cars in Holland.

Berka IWKA Armoured Vests

Germany

MODEL A
Weight: 6.3kg (with steel plate)
Weight Groin Protector: 2.5kg (with steel plate)

MODEL B
Weight: 7kg (without steel plate)
Weight Groin Protector: as for Model A

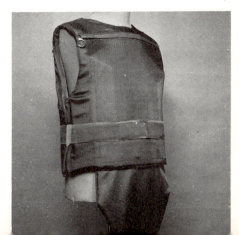

Right: IWKA armoured vest Model C.

MODEL C
Weight: 9kg (front steel plate 2.5kg, rear steel plate 3.5kg)

Development
Made of synthetic textile fibre, IWKA vests are extremely light. All models allow for the insertion of steel plates. Exhaustive tests carried out in Germany have shown that a high degree of protection is afforded. For instance an MP5 9mm was not able to penetrate the vest from 10m. The result was a dent diameter 10mm and maximum depth 1mm.

Employment
German Border Police (*Deutsche Bundesgrenzschutz*), police forces of several German states, several Swiss Cantonal police forces, and some German and foreign banks.

Hagor Armour Vest   Israel

Development
The Hagor Armour Vest is constructed of Kevlar, five times stronger by weight than steel. The outer shell of the vest consists of two layers of ballistic nylon. The vest is designed to give protection against an Uzi sub-machine gun fired from a distance of 10m.

Employment
Israeli Armed Forces.

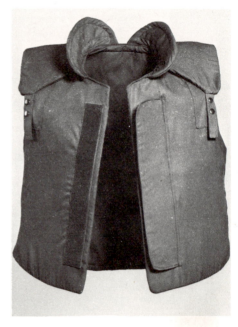

Right: *Hagor armour vest.*

TIG Bicord AG Armoured Vest and Helmet   Switzerland

Development
Developed for police and military use, this protective vest and headgear provides immunity against 9mm steel core ammunition and .357 Magnum rounds. Both vest and helmet have an outside layer of flame-resistant fabric, and therefore also protect the wearer against petrol bombs. Several types of vest are available.

Employment
Details not available.

TIG Bicord AG Bomb Disposal Suit   Switzerland

Development
Consisting of a protective helmet with wide-angle visor, front section, back protector panel and leg and foot protectors, this bomb disposal suit is made of extremely resistant material which largely eliminates potential injuries but allows good mobility. The front section incorporates an additional two-section metal armour plate of special ballistic material which is designed to deflect the shock wave in case the bomb explodes. The high collar provides protection against neck injuries, whilst the back section has a pocket for a radio transceiver and bomb disposal tools. The

helmet can be equipped with earphones and a microphone so that contact with the EOD specialist can be maintained. The wide-angle visor will stop a German 9mm Parabellum round fired from a pistol at any range.

Employment
Details not available.

Right: *TIG Bicord bomb disposal suit.*

Bristol Armour

UK

Development
Bristol Armour is formed from a fibre reinforced plastics composite to provide protection at varying levels (Grade 25-Grade 86) against low velocity weapons. A hard faced armour made of ceramic reinforced plastics is available to provide protection against armour piercing and high velocity bullets. Performance of grades is given below.

Grade 25: (max weight 5.31kg, front, back and pelvic)
Designed to stop 9mm ammunition fired from Sterling L2A3 sub-machine gun at 23m (75ft) range.

Grade 30: (max weight 5.46kg, front, back and pelvic)
Designed to stop 9mm parabellum ammunition fired from Browning automatic pistol at point blank range.

Grade 36: (max weight 7.41kg, front, back and pelvic)
Designed to stop .44 Magnum ammunition fired from 4in barrel revolver at 2.7m (9ft).

Grade 50: (max weight 10.11kg, front, back and pelvic)
Designed to stop .30 calibre ammunition fired from US M1 carbine at 32m (105ft).

Grade 64: (max weight 13.80kg, front back and pelvic)
Designed to stop 9mm armour-piercing steel cased ammunition fired from standard sub-machine guns at 5m (16ft).

Grade 86: (max weight 11.41kg, front and back only)
A hard faced armour designed to stop 7.62mm ball ammunition fired from FN FAL rifle at 91m (300ft).

Employment
Details not available.

Below: *Bristol armour.*

Bristol Composite Materials Armoured Clipboard   UK

Development
Developed by Bristol Composite Materials Engineering, the Armoured Clipboard is designed to give ballistic protection against hand guns at vehicle check points. It is an imaginative and highly practical development which, combined with body armour, should in most circumstances save lives.

Employment
Details not available.

Bristol Composite Materials Armoured Helicopter Seats   UK

Development
Bristol Composites supply a range of ceramic/fibre composite armour to protect helicopter crews from the effects of high velocity AP rounds. The armour, which can be designed to fit inside an existing crew seat or can be bolted on to the seat exterior, is available in a number of different grades. The heaviest of these is Grade 105A, capable of stopping multi-hits (at 5X calibre spacing) of 7.62mm AP ammunition from an FN FAL rifle at 90m range. Crew members can also be provided with breastplates of similar material.

Employment
British Army and RAF.

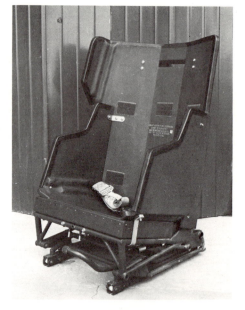

Right: *Puma helicopter armoured seat.*

Bristol Composite Materials Lightweight Helmet   UK

Development
The Bristol Lightweight Helmet is particularly suitable for IS work. The helmet is constructed in two grades of composites to give differing levels of protection. The Grade 9 helmet stops a 158 grain lead bullet fired from a Smith & Wesson .38 Special revolver at 5m at 260m/sec. The Grade 17 stops 17 grain fragments at 420m/sec. The Grade 9 weighs 0.75kg, the Grade 17 1.25kg.

Employment
Details not available.

Right: *Lightweight helmet with visor fitted.*

Bristol Concealed Armour

UK

Development
The armour consists of a basic Kevlar composite jacket weighing 1.55kg. It is claimed the vest stops .22, .38 Special, 357 Magnum, 9mm handguns and No 5 shot from 12 bore shotguns.

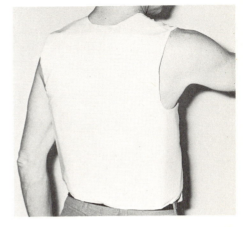

Right: *Bristol concealed armour.*

Bristol Flexible Armour

UK

Development
Bristol Flexible Armour is designed for over uniform wear and consists of a Kevlar composite jacket covering front, back and sides. Ceramic plates can be added to increase protection. The standard jacket weighs 3.9kg and the ceramic panels weigh 1.1kg, 2.2kg or 3.0kg each depending upon the level of protection afforded. The ceramic panels increase the protection to the level of 7.62 ammunition.

Employment
Details not available.

Right: *Bristol Flexible armour.*

Bristol Hard Armour Suit

UK

Development
Bristol have developed the Hard Armour Suit for wear by police or troops. The suit provides protection against NATO 7.62mm rounds, and consists of rear, front and front lower hard armour plates. It is particularly suitable for static tasks such as roadblocks, guarding vulnerable points, or for wear in a shoot-out.

Employment
Details not available.

Right: *Bristol hard armour suit.*

Bristol Transparent Armour
UK

Development

For use in military vehicles, and designed to stop low velocity ammunition, Bristol Transparent Armour weighs 43kg/m² at a thickness of 28mm.

Employment

Details not available.

Carleton Russell 'Armadillo' Bullet Resistant Laminate
UK

Development

Carleton Russell Ltd Armadillo is a lightweight, opaque bullet resistant laminate. The product is manufactured in layers of material each layer being approximately 0.63mm thick, and is built up in standard increments of five layers to a maximum of 60 layers. Only 9.45mm thickness Armadillo is required to resist three strikes by a 9mm handgun from a range of 3m, whereas 38mm thickness is required to withstand three strikes by a 7.62mm rifle from a range of 10m. Armadillo can be used for office or shop windows and police or VIP car windows.

Employment

Armadillo is in use in the United Kingdom and Holland.

Right: *Carleton Russell 'Armadillo' bullet resistant laminate after multi-strikes from 7.62 NATO rifle.*

Gault Glass Laminates EOD Suit
UK

Weight Jacket: 7.2kg
Weight Trousers: 3.8kg
Weight Back Apron: 3.6kg
Weight Breast and Pelvic Plates: 4.6kg

Development

Since trials with the British Army in 1974, the Gault Glass Laminates EOD Suit Mk 2 has entered production and further details have been made available. The suit, which weighs 19.2kg, comprises flexible-armour trousers and footshield extensions, flexible-armour jacket with high collar and back apron with two tool pockets in the skirt. To the front of the jacket is appended a rigid armour breastplate with integral deflector to direct blast away from the face and a rigid pelvic plate. Worn with the suit is a special heavyweight EOD helmet with armoured visor, developed by Amplivox (see page 64).

Employment

British Army.

MOD Body Armour
UK

FRAGMENTATION VEST, COLLAR AND ABDOMINAL PROTECTOR

This fragmentation protective vest is a development from an original US Army item and is intended to provide protection against fragmenting munitions for the neck, thorax and upper abdomen. The two pockets have been enlarged to accommodate a personal communication radio and non-slip patches are attached to each shoulder to prevent rifle butt slippage. The vest consists of an outer cover of textile which fastens at the front with a touch and close fastener and down the sides with adjustable lacing.

The filling consists of 16 plies of textile sewn together and stiffened with plastic sheeting. Total weight of the jacket is 4.11kg.

The Fragmentation Protective Collar is intended to be worn in conjunction with the fragmentation protective vest to give greater protection to the neck and lower part of the head against fragments from improvised explosive devices (IEDs). It was developed specifically for the use of members of teams searching for such devices.

The Abdominal Protector is a compulsory item to the Fragmentation Vest and Collar and is intended to protect the lower abdomen and pelvic areas against fragments from fragmenting munitions and improvised explosive devices and afford some

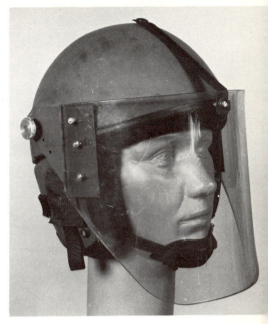

protection against blast. The vendor for Vest, Collar and Abdominal Protector is the UK Ministry of Defence (Sales).

Above left: *Fragmentation vest.* / Crown copyright

Above: *Prototype IED search helmet.* / Crown copyright

Employment
The Vest and Collar are in service with the British and US Armies, and the Abdominal Protector with the British Army only.

HELMET, ANTI-RIOT TRANSPORT (HART)
The ART Helmet is a commercial crash helmet to which has been added a transparent plastic visor to enable it to be used as an anti-riot helmet. The visor and helmet shell will give protection against hand thrown missiles but are not intended to provide ballistic protection. The helmet in addition provides a level of crash protection equivalent to that specified in BS 1869 (protective helmets for racing motor cyclists) for the protection of vehicle occupants.
The vendor is the UK Ministry of Defence (Sales).

Employment
British Army.

HELMET, IED SEARCH TEAMS
The helmet is intended to provide ballistic protection to members of teams searching for improvised explosive devices (IEDs) and explosives. The helmet will be similar in design to commercial crash helmets, but will have a ballistic protective shell moulded in a nylon or Kevlar textile/resin laminate. Ballistic protective visors of various thicknesses will be provided and audio gear for interfacing with communications systems and detection devices will be fitted. Removable plugs over the ears will aid

hearing when audio gear is not required. The Vendor is the UK Ministry of Defence (Sales).

Employment
The equipment is currently being developed for the British Army.

INTERNAL SECURITY COMBAT HELMET
Weight Helmet: 1.41kg
Weight Visor: 0.41kg

Development
The British Army has developed a new type of internal security helmet, known as the IS Combat Helmet. The helmet, which is made of composite material and incorporates a visor plus a new type of chinstrap liner, is lighter, more comfortable, more secure and gives a higher degree of ballistic protection than the general issue Mk 4 steel helmet. The wearer can also hear a great deal more easily than with the enclosed type HART (Helmet, Anti-Riot Transport) currently in service. The polycarbonate visor is readily detachable and a helmet cover can be added for operations in a rural environment.

Employment
British Army.

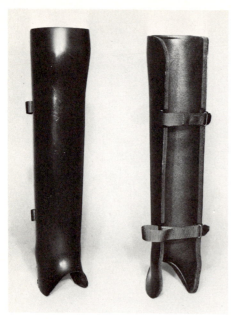

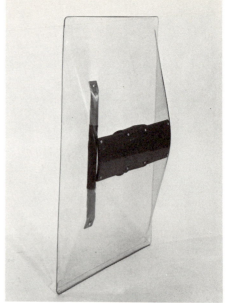

Above: *Protector, leg, anti-riot.* / Crown copyright

Above right: *Shield, anti-riot (moulded pattern).*

Right: *Suit, EOD Mk 2* / Crown copyright

PROTECTOR, LEG, ANTI-RIOT

The equipment is intended to protect the fronts of the lower legs from impacts of hand thrown missiles in riots. The protectors consist of thin moulded plastic sheets backed by polymer foam sheet to dissipate the energy of impact. The same pattern is used on both right and left legs and fastening to the legs is by means of two webbing straps passing behind the leg and secured by touch and close fasteners. The vendor is the UK Ministry of Defence (Sales).

Employment

British Army.

SHIELD ANTI-RIOT (MOULDED PATTERN)

The shield has been developed to afford protection against hand thrown missiles in riot situations without interfering in any way with the user's field of view. The shield consists of a moulded transparent plastic sheet with curled edge to promote greater rigidity and formed centre to provide a measure of side protection. The arm band has a touch and close fastening to enable quick release and the forearm is protected by a foam sheet to absorb impact energy. When in use the centre of gravity of the item falls inside the user's arm and thus prevents any torque being exerted on the arm. The equipment weighs 2.7kg. The vendor is the UK Ministry of Defence (Sales).

Employment

British Army.

SUIT EOD MK 2

Weight Suit: 14.6kg
Weight Helmet: 4.5kg
Weight Plates: 4.6kg

Development

The suit is intended to give protection against fragments, blast and flame to personnel involved in the disarming of small improvised explosive devices. It will also provide a measure of protection at greater ranges from larger devices. It is believed that the minimum requirement for the suit is that it should withstand a 250gm nail bomb exploding at a distance of 0.9m. The suit consists of a jacket, trousers and cape each containing a filler of a ballistic protective textile with a fire retardant textile cover. In the case of the jacket and cape the ballistic fillers are removable to aid laundering and in all three items the fillers are encased in PVC envelopes to exclude moisture which degrades ballistic performance. The jacket has a high collar providing protection for the neck and lower face and is provided at the front with two large pockets to accept reinforced plastic breast and pelvic plates which give added protection to the vital organs of the body. Pockets are provided on both the back of the suit and the cape to accept a radio and tools required in disposal operations. The jacket and trousers provide ballistic protection only at the front; the cape provides back protection if required. The helmet has a textile laminate shell and incorporates a sound excluding communications headset. The visor screen is a two part plastic system with intervening air gap.

Employment

British Army.

VARIABLE BODY ARMOUR

The British Army has recently adopted in limited quantities a new armoured jacket known simply as Variable Body Armour. Offering a considerably greater degree of protection against 7.62mm high velocity rounds than the 'flackjacket' at present in service, the VBA seen here worn by a soldier at a vehicle checkpoint, consists of a light protective jacket with pockets front and rear, into which heavy metal plates are inserted according to the degree of protection required. Weight considerations make it likely that the suit will be more usually worn by vehicle borne troops or those deployed in a semi-static role. Gross weight is 12kg. The vendor is the UK Ministry of Defence (Sales). The equipment is a modification of a US Army equipment.

Employment

US Army, British Army.

PDI Protector Shields

UK

Development

Manufactured by PDI of Birmingham from Lexan polycarbonate, the Protector Riot Shield is lightweight (3.18kg), transparent and tinted to reduce dazzle, and sufficiently flexible to deflect missiles. The peripheral gutter helps to disperse liquids hurled at the face. PDI also manufacture visors for anti-riot helmets.

Employment

PDI Anti-Riot Visors are used by the British Army.

Right: *PDI protector shields.*

Racal Amplivox EOD Helmet   UK

Weight: 4.7kg
Size: fits head lengths from 186mm to 207mm

Development

Manufactured from anti-ballistic material, the helmet
provides protection from blast and fragments, and is
fitted with Sonovalve acoustic valves to protect
against transient explosive noises. Full
communications facilities are also built in, including
a specially developed microphone with sound
conveyed via an acoustic tube incorporating a
sibilant filter and detachable background noise
attenuator, such that the system eliminates the
hazards of mounting a conventional boom
microphone in front of the wearer's face.

Employment

British Army.

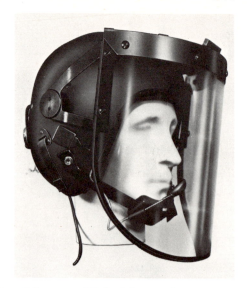

Right: *Racal Amplivox EOD helmet.*

SAS Developments SA12 Riot Visors, Shields and Helmets   UK

VISORS

The visors, made from 3mm thick polycarbonate, are
designed to fit the latest SA12 Riot Helmet, as well
as NATO and standard British Mk IV Steel Helmets,
although fittings suitable for any type of helmet can
be provided. All visors are supplied with a hinge
allowing them to be raised away from the wearer's
face when not in action. The clearance of the visor
from the wearer's face is such that the visor cannot
come into contact with his skin even if it is hit with a
wooden or iron bar. A 'stop' can be provided so that
the visor can be maintained in one or two alternative
raised positions.

SHIELDS

SA12 Shields are available in several different
shapes and designs. However, the standard shield is
913mm long, and 508mm wide, and weighs 2.25kg.
It has a shock absorbing foam rubber arm pad. The
shield is constructed of 3mm thick polycarbonate.

HELMETS

The standard helmet supplied specifically for riot
squads is manufactured from polycarbonate which is
of high impact grade and offers a high degree of
impact protection and penetration resistance,
coupled with an exceptional light weight. The helmet
shell will resist penetration by a spiked cylindrical
steel striker weighing 1.8kg dropped from a height of
two metres. The helmet will resist at least six blows
of 90ft-lbs impact (the equivalent of 0.46kg weight
dropped from 27.6m),

Employment

These equipments are in use with various armies and
police forces. In particular SAS visors are used by the
British Army on the Mk IV Steel Helmet.

Below: *SA12 helmet seen here with SA121
shockstick.*

Trevor Davies Hotspur Body Armour UK

Development
Utilising high performance Compass steel armour, the Hotspur Armoured Jacket is claimed to give much greater protection than those incorporating plastic or ceramic armours, as it does not lose its resistance to penetration under multiple impact. However, weight considerations limit protection to the main vulnerable body areas including heart, lungs and upper stomach. Detachable pelvic protectors can also be provided. The standard jacket uses 2.5mm armour and weighs 3.85kg, 4.99kg and 6.35kg in its small, medium and large sizes respectively. It defeats all handguns up to and including .357 Magnum, all 9mm and 0.45 SMGs in single shot or full burst at point blank range.

Variants
Hotspur also manufacture a 3kg Fragmentation Jacket.

Employment
Details not available.

Trevor Davies Hotspur Riot Shield UK

Development
The Hotspur Riot Shield is specifically designed for use by police and army personnel when faced with a situation where weapons other than firearms are likely to be used against them. Extremely light and comfortable to hold, the Hotspur Riot Shield can meet severe attack from knives, bricks, bottles and other missiles, as well as pick axe handles and clubs etc, easily available to the belligerent demonstrator. Complete protection from face to waist is offered by the shield, while at the same time allowing the maximum amount of vision. The carefully designed independent inner panel and arm groove reduce severe shock waves created by violent impact on the frontal panel to an absolute minimum. A firm and comfortable hand grip is fitted to the arm groove, and a quick release Velcro lining to the leather arm strap removes the possibility of broken or sprained arms when subject to sudden and severe twisting from the front.

Employment
Details not available.

Triplex Bullet Resistant Glass UK

Development
Violent attacks on VIP cars and security vehicles are increasing in frequency and ferocity all over the world. They re-emphasise the vital importance of drawing on modern security developments to provide maximum protection for vehicle occupants and valuables. Glass is of crucial importance. Road vehicles, especially saloons, must have adequate visibility; yet unprotected windows are highly vulnerable. However, these can be manufactured to offer a high degree of protection against handguns, shotguns and other weapons, and can even be curved and framed so that, when fitted, they are indistinguishable from ordinary glass. Triplex produce a range of tailored bullet resistant products designed to customer's specifications with additional features available such as Triplex Hyviz electro-conductive film for rapid de-misting, de-icing and for alarm systems. Special tints are also available offering varying degrees of colour density for control of solar transmission. Thus, the crews of payroll vans or military vehicles whose work puts them at risk of violent attack, and VIPs who have to travel in sensitive areas, can be protected.

Employment
A variety of private customers in South America and the Middle East employ Triplex glass on private motor cars. In addition the glass is fitted to the Shorts Armoured car used by the Royal Ulster Constabulary and to the GKN AT-104 armoured patrol vehicles.

Vacuum Research Camsafe Shatter Resistant Film UK

Development
An increasingly used method of combating the problem of flying glass caused by a terrorist bomb is the use of shatter resistant film, which, when applied to a window, holds the particles of glass together after breaking and restricts the scatter of glass fragments. Camsafe, developed by Vacuum Research Ltd, when applied to glass is virtually undetectable and once the adhesive has set in approximately 14 days forms a strong glass to film laminate. Camsafe is based on Melinex polyester film supplied by ICI. It has been tested under explosions of different magnitudes, and in all these tests the shattered glass was held together by the film and glass fragments were restrained.

Employment
Camsafe is in use in the United Kingdom, and several other countries.

Left: *The result of an explosion on untreated glass showing glass fragments flying from the window frame.*

Below left: *The result of an explosion on a treated window where the extreme force of a large explosion has projected the complete treated glass piece out of the frame. In this case however the glass sheet only travels a short distance from the frame and is kept intact.*

Volumatic Anti-Bomb Curtains

UK

Development
Developed by Volumatic in conjunction with Filigree Textiles Ltd of Nottingham, the net curtaining is designed to the specification laid down by the UK Department of the Environment's Property Services Agency for the protection of its own buildings. The purpose of the curtains is to prevent flying glass resulting from an explosion causing serious injury. The bottom of the curtain is weighted to the extent of 400g per metre width.

Employment
United Kingdom Department of the Environment.

Right: *Volumatic anti-bomb curtains.*

Armour of America Sacramento Vest   USA

Development

Developed by Armour of America of Beverly Hills, the Sacramento Vest is designed for use by police and SWAT teams. It is designed to hold chest and back panels of any grade of hard armour; it is a sleeveless garment reinforced with ballistic nylon felt which acts as a shock absorber when hit by rocks and bottles, so it is also ideal for crowd control. Without an insert the Sacramento Vest can stop 9mm sub-machine gun fire at 8m, and weighs 4.08kg (SAC AHP Version). A Sacramento Armour Shield insert weighing an additional 2.88kg will stop a 7.62 NATO round at 8m. The garment also provides protection for the neck, spine and groin.

Employment

Various US SWAT teams and police forces.

Armour of America Tactical Vest   USA

Development

The Armour of America Tactical Vest, without a hard armour insert, can stop a 9mm sub-machine gun at 8m. With an insert of Bristol Armour, the Tactical Vest can stop up to 30.06 AP. The vest is available in two versions, the AJ weighing 4.54kg, and the AHP weighing 2.72kg.

Employment

Various US police forces.

Right: *Armour of America Tactical vest.*

Armour of America Undershirt Armoured Vest   USA

Development

Armour of America has developed a range of lightweight vests for undershirt wear. These provide protection against most handguns, and include Armour-Hide (1.1kg), Super Armour-Hide (1.7kg), Super Armour-Hide Contour (1.81kg), Armour-Hide Super Contour + P (1.5kg) and Ultra-thin (0.89kg). The Armour-Hide range offer slightly differing levels of protection, but all are of the same basic design.

Employment

Various US police forces.

Armour of America Woman's Vest

USA

Left: *Armour of America woman's vest.*

Development

The Armour of America Women's Vest is designed for policewomen and can stop virtually all hand guns including .38 calibre, 9mm HP and .41 Magnum. It weighs 0.91kg, and is available in chest sizes 32, 34, 36 and 38.

Variants

The women's vest is available in a version providing a slightly higher degree of protection against 9mm FMJ (USA) and weighing 1.1kg.

Employment

Various US police forces.

Burlington Body Armour

USA

Above: *Burlington riot jacket.*

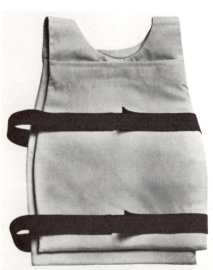

Above: *Burlington bullet resistant vest.*

RIOT JACKET

Designed for protection during riots, the Burlington Riot Jacket is made of ballistic nylon. It provides protection against .38 and .45 (lead nose) projectiles. The jacket weighs approximately 5.5kg.

TAC JACKET

The Tac Jacket provides full coverage of the front, back and sides of the upper torso, as well as the shoulders, all at high protection levels. The jacket is constructed of Kevlar and PM-1300, a specially treated material developed by Protective Materials Co to reduce blunt trauma. These materials allow the Tac Jacket to defeat all handguns, shotguns and sub-machine guns up to and including the .44 Magnum, and most 9mm ammunition. A front pouch is provided to accommodate an Assault Plate, which protects the vital organs from frontal attack up to and including the 30.06 armour piercing projectile.

BULLET RESISTANT VESTS

Burlington Bullet Resistant Vests are designed for wear underneath clothing. The 7840 is made of ballistic nylon.

Employment

New Orleans, Philadelphia and Chicago Police departments.

Burlington Bombthret Suits   USA

Development

Weighing 16kg, the PA-800 Bombthret Suit provides a high level of protection for vital organs and major arteries against blast, fragmentation and chemical spray. The arms are unemcumbered to permit maximum freedom of motion.

Variants

The PA-810A employs the same ballistic nylon leg protection, but substitutes a ballistic helmet, polycarbonate face mask and separate armoured torso and groin pieces for the one piece head and torso unit of the PA-800.

Employment

Various US police departments.

Right: *The PA-800 (left) and PA-810A (right) Bombthret suits.*

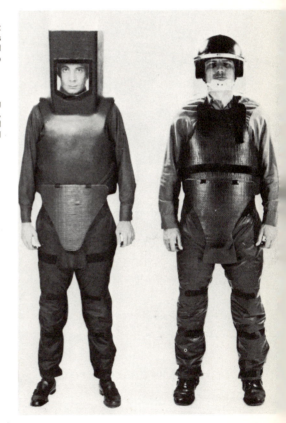

Second Chance Body Armour   USA

Development

Hardcorps I, developed by Second Chance Body Armour of Central Lake, Michigan, weighs 8.8kg and is designed for use by IS forces. Second Chance claim it will stop an AK-47 7.62mm armour-piercing round at one metre range, as well as all handguns, shotguns and sub-machine guns. Hardcorps III is a concealable version, which Second Chance claim has the same ballistic resistance as Hardcorps I. It is designed for wear by plain-clothes police, IS personnel and VIPs. Second Chance claim that Hardcorps III and Model Z9 and Model Y variants saved the lives of 81 policemen in the US up to October 1976. Weight is 6.4kg.

Employment

Second Chance Body Armour is used by some 50 Police Departments in the US, including the San Francisco, Detroit and Chicago Police, the Texas, Ohio, Massachussetts Police Departments, the Michigan State Police, and the FBI.

Sierra SWAT Ballistic Helmets   USA

MODEL SD357

Weighing 1.91kg, the SD357 Ballistic Helmet has been developed by the Sierra Engineering Co of Sierra Madre for use by police and anti-terrorist personnel to provide protection against .357 calibre handguns fired from a range of three metres. The helmet is provided with a chinstrap and visor.

MODEL GP380

Weighing only 1kg, the GP380 Ballistic Helmet provides protection against .38 calibre handguns fired from a range of three metres.

Employment

Various US police forces.

Left: *SD357 Ballistic helmet.*

Sierra Body Armour   USA

Development

Sierra has produced a 1.6kg assault body armour jacket for wear in all combat situations. Its low weight makes it very suitable for use by IS forces for patrolling in urban or rural areas.

Employment

Various US police departments.

Smith & Wesson Protective Equipment   USA

MODEL 68 HELMET

Specially designed for riot duty, the Smith & Wesson Model 68 Helmet is constructed of pressure moulded glass fibre with polyester resin. The removable visor permits attachment of a face shield which can be worn with the Model 67 Smith & Wesson Riot Gas Mask.

BARRIER VEST BODY ARMOUR

The Model 217 Barrier Vest Body Armour contains ballistic steel protection in both the front and the back. Seven layers of barrier cloth are bonded to the steel at the back, and ten layers at the front. Without the detachable groin protector the Model 217 weighs 4kg. The groin protector weighs 1kg.

Employment

Various US police departments.

Section IV: Bomb Disposal Equipment

The most widely used terrorist weapon is the bomb. The international incidence of this weapon in recent years has been depressingly frequent. Most nations now have Explosive Ordnance Disposal (EOD) teams. These teams have available to them various bomb disposal aids. In particular remotely controlled vehicles, capable of carrying and operating a variety of equipment necessary for the location and disposal of dangerous objects, have been developed. These vehicles enable the EOD expert to remain at a safe distance while he locates and identifies by means of a TV camera and monitor the suspected bomb. If he judges that the object is too dangerous to be approached he can attempt to disarm or destroy it using various means on the remotely controlled vehicle. To date only the US and the UK have entered this field to an appreciable degree. However this monopoly is unlikely to last much longer.

It would be wrong to suggest that the remotely controlled vehicle is the total answer to the EOD man's problem. Manual approaches are still the only answer in certain circumstances. Indeed experience in the UK has shown that manual approaches are still necessary in approximately 40% of cases.

Allen Type HAL EOR Hook and Line Set — UK

Right: *Allen hook and line set Type HAL.*

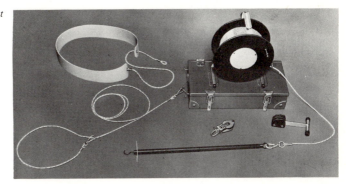

Development

Each set consists of a reel holding 100 metres of line mounted on a very strong steel case which contains a selection of lines, hooks, strops, extension rods, pulling handles and snatch blocks. This set which weighs 19kg, has been developed by P. W. Allen & Co to assist trained EOR/EOD operatives in moving and/or lifting IEDs or other potentially hazardous objects. The equipment is compact so that is may easily be carried in service vehicles. A carrying handle enables it to be transported by one man. Case dimensions are 51cm x 25.5cm x 11.5cm.

Employment

Details not available.

Allen Type EOD Inspection Set — UK

Development

Developed by P. W. Allen of London, the Inspection Set Type EOD is designed to assist EOD operatives in the internal inspection of IEDs of all kinds including parcels, packages, cases, luggage and also inside locks, particularly where forensic evidence is required. Components are made of non-ferrous metals, and include various light probes, extension rods, round mirrors, a recovery magnet and hook, lock viewers, and illuminated inspection mirrors. Dimensions of the case are 61cm x 48cm x 7cm, and the total weight of the equipment is 5kg.

Employment

This equipment is used by the British Army and many other operators throughout the world.

Right: *Allen inspection set EOD.*

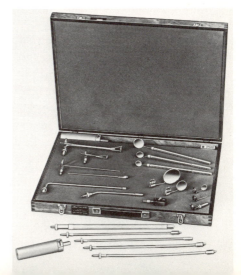

Allen EOD Safety Light Probe UK

Development

Developed by P. W. Allen, the EOD Safety Light Probe is a hand held battery operated light source with a 15.2cm long x 3mm diameter fibre optic light probe. The lamp is totally enclosed in the handle and the light, which is 'piped' into the object being inspected by the fibre optic probe, is therefore cold (and safe).

Employment

This equipment is in service with the British Army and many other operators throughout the world.

Left: *Allen safety light probe Type SLP.*

Allen SE30 Mk 2 Search Endescope UK

Total length: 3.08m (also usable in lengths of .68m, 1.28m, 1.88m and 2.48m)
Diameter: 3cm
Weight: 12kg

Right: *Allen search endescope SE30 (Mk II).*

Development

The SE30 Endescope (or Periscope) developed by P. W. Allen of London is designed to assist arms/contraband search teams in searching normally inaccessible places. It is made up in seven sections:

one ocular (or eyepiece) tube, two objective tubes (one for direct forward viewing and one for lateral viewing) and four extension tubes. Tungsten/halogen lamps are housed in the objective tubes. The equipment is able to focus from a few cms to infinity with great depth at any setting. The SE30 is particularly suitable for searching buildings, vehicles or ships without breaking walls, ceilings or floorboards or offloading vehicles or removing panels or container sides from ships.

Variants

The Allen Search Endoscope SE737 is an unilluminated hand-held endoscope designed for use by infantry patrols searching buildings. With a 65° angle of view and alternative direct forward or 90° viewing the SE37 enables an operator to see the whole of a room through a hole only 20mm in diameter. This includes all the back of the door or wall through which the equipment is placed. No focussing is required. The SE737 is 51cm in length and 19mm in diameter. The case dimensions are 60cm x 4.5cm.

Employment

These equipments are in use with the British Army and in many other countries throughout the world.

Hunter Remote Control EOD Vehicle UK

Right: *SAS Hunter bomb disposal robot.*

Vehicle Weight: 115kg
Vehicle Width: .65m
Length: 1.25m
Operational Height: 1.3m (with boom raised)
Speed: 30m/min approx
Range: 100m
Endurance: 2hr approx
Power Supply: 2 x24v integral batteries

Development

A joint Hunting Engineering and SAS Group venture, the remotely controlled Hunter robot was developed by experienced EOD officers to be as flexible and simple to operate as possible. Special features include an exceptional degree of control at slow speeds, constant power at all speeds, single fingertip control, and an articulated arm mounting for both shotgun and disrupters. The equipment is intended for use in a wide range of operations in addition to its primary EOR/EOD role, eg fire fighting, anti-hijack, natural disasters and hostage situations. Extra capability available includes radio control, foam delivery, X-ray and an electronic stethoscope. Standard attachments are car hook, scissors grip, grapnel, scoop, nail gun, and tilting arm (mounting shotgun/disrupter, window breaker, charge dropper, camera panning unit).

Employment

The system is in use with many military organisations throughout the world.

Morfax Marauder Bomb Disposal Equipment   UK

Width: .648m
Length: 1.41m (idlers down)
.736m (idlers up)
Length (for storage): 1.219m
Max Height: 863m (arms down)
2.54m (arms up)
Max Speed: 65cm/sec
Power Supply: 2 x 12v 50amp on board batteries

Development

Developed as a potential successor to Wheelbarrow, the British Army's current bomb disposal remote handling aid, Marauder has demonstrated a significantly improved stair-climbing capability and, having variable track geometry, is capable of manoeuvring in smaller spaces, both features being a distinct advantage when operating in buildings.

Marauder has a central television arm which can be swung through a 110° arc, plus an arm for mounting weapons (shotgun, nail gun, disrupter, etc) and a manipulator arm for unwrapping packages and unlocking doors. The latter two arms also have their own individual CCTV camera and lighting equipments (though only two out of the three cameras can be utilised simultaneously) and being multi-joint construction can manoeuvre through 180°. The operator observes the equipment via twin portable monitors and is linked to it via 150m of lightweight cable. Radio remote control is also feasible, which would give an extended range capability.

Employment

Details not available.

Morfax Wheelbarrow Mk 7 Bomb Disposal Equipment   UK

Left: *Wheelbarrow showing boom mounting camera.*

Vehicle Weight: 195kg (Operational)
Vehicle Width: .69m
Length: 1.22m
Min Operational Height: .82m (with boom folded)
Speed: 33.5m/min
Range: 100m (standard cable and drum)
Endurance: 2hr (mean)
Power supply: 2 x 12v 50A/hr lead/acid batteries
Closed Circuit TV Camera: Single lens (240v 50Hz) supplied via an invertor
Monitor: 9in model (12v DC or 240v 50Hz)

Development

The Mk 7 Wheelbarrow is the latest version of a concept which first saw operational service in 1972. It was developed in order to perform many of the functions which previously placed members of IS forces at considerable risk, and is capable of handling a variety of equipment necessary for the locating and disposal of potentially dangerous objects. The vehicle is powered by two reversible electric motors, running off inboard 24 volt batteries. The vehicle carries vertical and horizontal booms for locating various manipulating items. The Wheelbarrow has a remotely controlled CCTV camera and panning head, allowing the operator to control his vehicle, from a safe position using a TV monitor. Commands are transmitted to the vehicle by means of a detachable 100m 18-way control cable. The EOD operator can now attack virtually any Improvised Explosive Device (IED) he encounters, and if he runs out of time it is a machine that is damaged, not a man killed. However, experience has shown that rarely is a Wheelbarrow totally destroyed in an explosion. The application of

Wheelbarrow is not limited to EOD work. With the multi-pupose central mount (MPCM) it can carry and automatically fire a variety of weapons used in riot, hostage or 'shoot-out' situations.

Variants
There is a comprehensive range of attachments available for Wheelbarrow.

Employment
Various US police forces, British Army.

SAS Developments SA91 Disrupter and Cartridge   UK

Length: 2.7cm
Diameter: 3.7cm
Weight: .44kg
Water Capacity: 100cc

Development
The SA91 disrupter and its associated cartridges make use of space technology and explosive ordnance disposal experience to produce a really lightweight but effective method of dealing with most normal types of improvised explosive device. Although it only weighs 440g and is filled with plain water, the SA91, when initiated either on the ground, or from a remotely controlled system, has proved to be thoroughly effective against terrorist explosive devices.

Above: *SA91 disrupter.*

Employment
Details not available

Volumatic Bomb Suppression Blanket   UK

Development
Made of a specially designed ballistic nylon with fire resistant coating, the Volumatic Bomb Suppression Blanket will contain blasts from home made bombs of varying size and design. Its 16sq ft of coverage provides full protection, yet the blanket is light enough (25lb) to be carried by one man. In high

magnitude explosions, the blanket rises to a parachute configuration, while the sides drop, so containing the blast.

Employment
The Bomb Blanket has been supplied to the Governments of Zambia, Libya and South Africa.

Burlington Bomb Blanket   USA

Right: *Burlington bomb blanket.*

Development

The Burlington Industrial Fabrics Co has developed a bomb blanket which is constructed of ballistic nylon, measures 2m x 2m, and weighs 27kg. Burlington claim that the blanket has effectively suppressed the explosive force of a pipe bomb charged with .35kg of smokeless pistol powder. In further tests, using three sticks of 60% dynamite, it has contained the explosion with minimal damage to the building in which the test took place.

Employment

Details not available.

PA-B300 Bombthret Sled   USA

Development

To minimise personnel exposure during the approach and initial handling of suspected explosive devices, Protective Materials Company of Andover, Massachusetts, has developed a bomb handling sled. This shield is designed to deflect the blast and fragmentation likely to be encountered should the suspect device detonate prior to being placed in a secure container. The sled chassis is mounted on locking swivel casters in the rear and rigid casters in front, which allows free movement on virtually all floor surfaces. The shield face, sides and bottom are constructed of PM-1200 armour material. The large viewpoint is a transparent non-fragmenting composite designed to equal the ballistic capability of the shield. The shield face is curved and severely canted rearward. 'U' slots are provided at the top of the shield face to allow operation of telescoping a prosthetic tool for lifting and placement of the suspect device.

Employment

Details not available.

PA-600 Bombthret Blanket   USA

Development

Made of specially designed ballistic nylon with fire resistant coating, the Bombthret Blanket will contain explosions from a large variety of bombs. Sixteen square feet of coverage provides substantial protection, yet the Bombthret Blanket is light enough (11.3kg) to be carried by one man. In high magnitude explosions, the blanket rises to a parachute configuration while the sides drop to contain the blast. In the event of an overmatch, the Bombthret Blanket will 'fail safe', that is, it will not contribute any additional hazard.

It is manufactured by the Protective Materials Co of Andover, Massachusetts.

Employment

Details not avialable.

PA-T-200 Bomb Disposal Trailer   USA

Towing Vehicle: Automobile or light truck
Weight: 2,631kg (with sand)
Brakes: Electric or hydraulic surge type available
Length: 3.25m
Width: 2.13m
Height: 1.72m
Speed: Can be safely towed at 70mph
Capacity: Safely vents 50 sticks of 40% dynamite
Containment Vessel: Double walled and double bottom stress-relieved, full penetration welds

Development

The Protective Materials Co of Andover, Massachusetts, has developed the T-200 Bomb Disposal Trailer for the transportation of suspected bombs, near critical volatile substances, or dangerous chemicals. The trailer carries the suspected bomb in a net suspension system. If any explosion should occur, the blast is vented upward and away from the towing vehicle and its crew. The trailer has a remote loading system to place the suspected bomb in the carrying net.

Variants

The T-100 Bomb Disposal Trailer is designed to be towed by almost any car or light truck.

Employment

Various US police forces.

Chem-Devil Bomb Disposal System   USA

Development

The Chem-Devil project originated in September 1974 when the Munitions Support Directorate, Picatinny Arsenal delivered a trailer-mounted determine the feasibility of using modified M113-A1 APCs in a hazardous munitions disposal operation at Dugway Proving Ground in Utah. After concept feasibility was established in November 1974, the design and construction of two systems was initiated, and seven months later the units were completed and shipped to Dugway Proving Ground. The vehicles are now in daily service and are operating at or beyond their design parameters. A highly modified commercial hydraulic loader crane has been mounted on the inner floor and extends through a specially designed 360° flexible seal mounted in the roof. The crane has a reach of 8.2m and a lifting capacity of 226.8kg. Two TV cameras are provided for continuous viewing of disposal operations by the crew. A ballistic window is also provided for direct viewing. The control console incorporates features which permit the crane operator to drive the vehicle. The crew compartment has been fitted with air conditioning and air filtration systems. Both vehicles have been coated with a highly reflective white urethane paint to reduce crew compartment temperature and to keep the outside surface free of hazardous substances. Radio communication between both vehicles and a command post and TV transmission systems are part of the on-board electronics.

Employment

Although both vehicles are currently employed at Dugway Proving Ground in the US, they are available for use by police or army units.

Total Containment Bomb Trailer   USA

Development

In 1976 the Munitions Support Directorate at Picatinny Arsenal delivered a trailer mounted explosive blast containment vessel to the FBI Bomb Data Program. The vessel is spherical to withstand explosive forces with minimum wall thickness and to equalise these forces in all directions so that relatively lightweight support and trailer suspension can be used. The vessel is a 91.4cm diameter steel sphere with approx 1.9cm wall thickness and includes a 45.7cm diameter opening with externally hinged door. A replaceable centring support is furnished to position the explosive inside the sphere and a captive net can be used remotely to emplace the explosive into the vessel and then remove it remotely at the disposal site. The complete assembly weighs approximately 544.3kg.

Employment

The Total Containment Bomb Trailer is used by the FBI in the United States.

Below: *Total containment bomb trailer developed by the Munitions Support Directorate at Picatinny Arsenal.*

Section V: Detection Equipment

One of the main tasks of troops and police engaged in IS duties is the checking of vehicles and their occupants. Another frequent task is the searching of houses and waste ground. In the same way airport security personnel have to keep a constant watch for attempts by terrorists to smuggle IEDs or weapons on to aeroplanes. Various equipments have been developed to detect metal objects on the person or in luggage, or explosive substances. Most explosive 'sniffers' will positively identify and indicate the presence of gelignite, dynamite, nitro-glycerine, nitro-benzine, and numerous other types of explosives. This section will include explosive 'sniffers', metal detectors for use about the person, and some airport X-ray equipment. Conventional mine/metal detectors for use on the ground will not be included, though these are used in IS situations.

Balteau Bactobloc X-Ray Equipment   Belgium

Total Weight: 98kg
Cupboard Depth: 60cm
Cupboard Width: 48cm
Cupboard Height: 40cm
Chamber Door Aperture: 50cm x 32cm

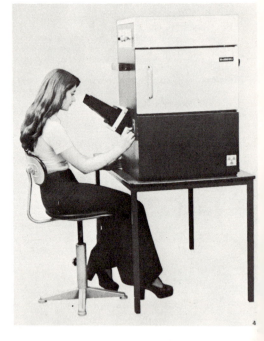

Development

The Bactobloc SPO70 is a simple and complete radioscopy equipment developed by Balteau of Beyne-Hensay for the rapid inspection of various objects and packages. The Bactobloc SPO70 (and the larger SPO100 model) are mainly suitable for the examination of light metals, plastics, organic materials, aluminium, electronic components, integrated circuits, wood, rubber, paper, small animals, etc. This equipment is primarily designed for the inspection of packages and mail addressed to ministries, embassies, banks, prisons, etc., though it has other uses in factories and laboratories.

Variants

The Bactobloc SPO120, 140, 160 and 200 models are designed more especially for the examination of denser materials, such as ceramics, castings, welds, explosives, etc.

Employment

Details not available.

Right: *Balteau Bactobloc SPO70 X-Ray equipment.*

Balteau Postix Letter Bomb Detector   Belgium

Total Weight: 70kg
Depth: 54.6cm
Width: 50.6cm
Height: 45cm
Aperture for Introduction of Mail: 5cm x 27.5cm

Development

Developed by Balteau for the examination of mail, it is only necessary to insert envelopes through a lateral aperture and then observe its radioscopic image on a screen. When in use the equipment is placed on a table where it occupies not much more space than a typewriter. It comprises a small X-ray

Right: *Balteau Postix*

generator, a radioscopy system, with screen and observation eye-shade and a small motorised manipulator which is controlled by the operator and enables the objects under examination to be passed before the screen.

Employment

This equipment is in use in various government establishments in Belgium and elsewhere in Europe.

Balteau Viewix X-Ray Equipment   Belgium

Development

The Viewix is a portable televised radioscopy system enabling suspect objects to be observed at a distance from where they have been deposited. It enables the contents of these objects to be seen and may help to determine the safest ways in which they can be neutralised. It consists of a small aluminium case which is light and easily portable, completely enclosed and light-tight , and a TV monitor . Within the case two fluorescent screens are placed back-to-back, one on the front face and the other on a lateral wall . An ultrasensitive television camera observes one screen or the other, according to the position given to a pivoting mirror by an external control . For using the

equipment, the most convenient of the walls covered internally by fluorescent screens is placed against the suspect object and is connected by cable to the TV monitor which is situated at a distance. A portable X-ray generator is placed on the other side of the suspect object. The control of this generator is situated near the TV monitor, to which it is connected by cable. As soon as the X-ray generator is started up, the radioscopic image of the object, which appears on the fluourescent screen, is transmitted by the camera to the monitor, where it can be observed in safety.

Employment

Details not available.

Leigh Marsland Model S201 Explosives Detector   Canada

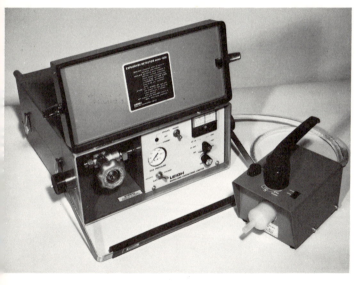

Left: *Leigh Marsland Engineering explosives detector Model S201.*

Total Weight of Equipment: 11.8kg
Depth of Main Unit: 43.4cm
Width of Main Unit: 33.2cm
Height of Main Unit: 15.2cm
Depth of Probe: 21.6cm
Width of Probe: 13cm
Height of Probe: 10.2cm
Response Time: 3sec
Gas Supply: Sufficient for 60hr continuous use

Development

Leigh Marsland Engineering of Waterloo, Ontario,

has developed the S201 vapour detector which is designed to sense vapours from a broad range of civil and military manufactured explosives. Powered by rechargeable nickel-cadmium batteries, the 10kg main unit can easily be carried by hand or on a back pack. Audio and visual alarms are provided.

Employment

Canadian Armed Forces.

Leigh Marsland Model S301 Explosives Detector Canada

Total Weight of Equipment: 249kg
Depth of Caster Mounted Units: 76.2cm (not including ramps)
Overall Width of Caster Mounted Units: 1.83m
Gateway Width of Caster Mounted Units: 68.6cm
Overall Height of Caster Mounted Units: 2.032m

Development

The Leigh Marsland Model S301 vapour detector is an electronic device which will detect explosives hidden on a person's body or on his clothing. As the individual passes through a doorway, a curtain of air sweeps vapours from the body and into the detectors, any one of which will detect the presence of explosives. To function reliably the individual should pause for three seconds in the air curtain. This device required six seconds to process an individual; a hand held detector requires 20-50 seconds.

Employment

Canadian Government.

Right: *Leigh Marsland Engineering explosives detector Model S301.*

Outokumpu Metor Weapon Detector Finland

Electronic Cabinet Weight: 14kg
Coil Weight: 270kg
Cabinet Depth: 35cm
Cabinet Width: 50cm
Cabinet Height: 18.5cm
Coil Max Depth: 2.35m
Coil Max Width: 1.27m
Coil Max Height: 2.308m

Below: *Outukumpu Metor weapon detector.*

Development

Outokumpu Oy of Espoo has developed a highly successful weapon detector designed primarily for use at airports. When a metal object causes an alarm, a red lamp will light up either on the front panel of the cabinet or on a remote visual alarm display unit. The alarm signal can also be used to activate door locks. The system sensitivity is variable, this determining the minimum size of object to be detected.

Employment
The equipment is in use mostly at airports, but also in other roles in Angola, Argentina, Canada, Denmark, Finland, Greece, Hungary, Iran, Italy, Jordan, Luxembourg, Malawi, Netherlands, Nigeria, Norway, Saudi Arabia, Spain, Switzerland, Taiwan, Tanzania, the USA, and Venezuela.

Institut Dr Forster Ferex 4.021 Search Instrument

Germany

Right: *Ferex 4.021.*

Dimensions Carrying Case:
1.11m x 14.5cm x 27cm
Dimensions Power Supply Unit:
9.5cm x 5.5cm x 31.5cm
Dimensions Control Unit: 9.5cm x 10cm x 26cm
Dimensions Probe Tube:
60cm long, diameter 4.6cm
Dimensions Carrying Tube: 1.035m long
Weight: 4.5kg (ready for operation)
Locating Range: 6m

Development
Developed by the Institut Dr Forster of Reutlingen, the Ferex 4.021 is more than a conventional mine detector, and particularly suitable for IS conditions. The probe can be used with or without the carrying tube, and also for searching underwater up to a depth of 30m. The device measures the degree of interference caused by a ferro-magnetic object by means of a differential-field measuring arrangement.

Employment
German Bundeswehr.

Vallon Models MH1603 and MH1604 Metal Detectors

Germany

	MH1603	MH1604
Length	39cm	40cm
Weight	.5kg	.45kg

Development
The MH1603 and 1604 have been developed by Vallon of Reutlingen to provide security forces with a convenient metal detector capable of performing checks on persons and packages. In the field this equipment has been used to detect ammunition hidden in tree-trunks, hedgerows, behind walls and other similar hiding places. Both variants use a 9v battery.

Employment
West German Police, Bundeskriminalamt and Landeskriminalamt, West German Army, Lufthansa.

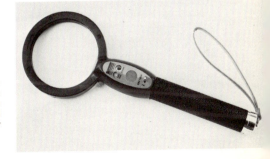

Above: *Vallon metal detector Model MH1604.*

81

Vallon Model MP1781 Metal Detector   Germany

Electronic Cabinet Weight: 14.5kg
Gate (including foot bridge) Weight: 87kg
Cabinet Depth: 28cm
Cabinet Width: 49cm
Cabinet Height: 18cm
Gate Depth: 39cm
Gate Width: 91cm
Gate Height: 2.16m

Development

The Vallon metal detector was developed for use in airports, and provides a visual alarm signal when any metal object passes through the gateway.

Variants

The model MP1770 metal detector employs the same gate and footbridge but has a slightly more sophisticated electronic cabinet, which indicates on which part of the body a metal object is secreted.

Employment

West German Airport Authority, Luftansa.

Left: *Vallon metal detector Model MP1771.*

Riwosa MD-12 Metal Detector   Switzerland

Weight: 1.760kg
Length: 40cm

Development

Developed by Riwosa of Zurich for detecting weapons or other metallic objects, this equipment has sold in large quantities. It operates on three 9v batteries.

Employment

British MOD, London Metropolitan Police, British Home Office, British Atomic Energy Commission, British Foreign and Commonwealth Office, British Department of the Environment, Iraqi Army, Kenya MOD, and Hong Kong, Indian, Pakistan and Taiwan Governments; also the police forces of Nigeria, Oman, Barbados, Gibraltar, Seychelles, Antigua, and Sharjah, and the security sections of British Airways, Air Canada, Air France, British West Indian Airways, China Airlines Ltd, Malaysian Airlines, National Airlines, Quantas Airways, Zambia Airways, Thai International Airline, and Singapore Airlines.

Right: *Riwosa metal detector MD-12 in use with experts of the Royal Army Ordnance Corps of the British Army.*

Riwosa Quick Alarm

Switzerland

The Riwosa Quick Alarm enables security guards, policemen, or personnel of the armed forces to transmit a call for help invisibly to a central alarm centre. A switch-on insert located in the shoe enables the wearer to activate the emitter. The switch-on system is so designed as to permit its use with practically any type of 'walkie-talkie'. Thus, not only is the alarm centre alerted, but all conversations are also transmitted, thus revealing the extent of the emergency.

Variants

For the security of particularly vulnerable personnel a miniaturised emitter (rather than the 'walkie-talkie') can be attached by a suspender or wire holder to the individual to be protected.

Employment

Details not available.

Add-on Electronics B-100 Metal Detector

UK

Diameter: 21.6cm
Height: 10.2cm
Weight: 0.59kg

Development

Add-on Electronics of Edenbridge developed this high sensitivity metal detector for the detection of all ferrous and non ferrous metals. It was primarily designed for airport security and police work, although there are numerous uses in the commercial field.

Employment

Thai Army, British Army, German police.

Right: *Add-On Electronics B-100 metal detector.*

Add-on Electronics IPD/2S Metal Detector

UK

Weight: 454g
Length: 36cm
Battery Life: 2-3 months with average daily use

Development

Complementary to the Add-on Electronics B100 hand detector (see above), the IPD/2S is suitable for searching personnel, baggage, walls, floors, etc for metal objects such as arms and ammunition. The IPD/2S is also widely used for screening mail for indications of explosive devices, and is capable of detecting very small metal parts, including those made of stainless and austenitic steel.

Variants

The IPD/2L has a longer stem (51cm) and the weight is increased to 539g. The longer stem enables the front and back to be searched without either the person being searched or the operator having to turn or move around.

Employment

The IPD/2S is in use in no less than 107 countries. These include Spain, Morocco, West Germany, Finland, the Republic of China, Thailand, Holland, Norway, South Africa, Nigeria, India, Japan and Hong Kong.

Right: *Add-On Electronics 1PD-2S metal detector.*

Allen Model A33 Fluorescent Hand Lamp   UK

Development

Designed by P. W. Allen of London specially for IS
work, the Model A33 produces a flood of white light
over a large area and is particularly suitable for
mobile search teams operating at night. The lamp
uses a 22.9cm fluorescent tube powered by a 12v
dry battery. One battery will give over eight hours
continuous operation, and well over 30 hours with
normal intermittent use. The light provided by the
lamp is comparable to that from a 40-watt tungsten
lamp.

Employment

Various security organisations in the UK.

Right: *Allen fluorescent hand lamp Type A33.*

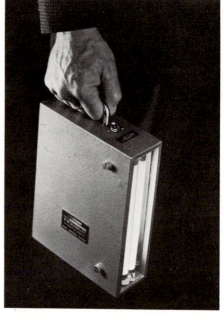

Allen Type VM Under-Vehicle Inspection Mirror   UK

Left: *Allen Type VM
under-vehicle inspection
mirror.*

Development

Inspection of the undersides of motor vehicles — for security or servicing, is one of the many applications for the Allen Type VM Illuminated Inspection Mirror. It comprises a thick 30.4cm convex mirror and 22.8cm fluorescent tube mounted on a base fitted with a detachable handle. A ball-caster provides easy manoeuvrability. Power source for outside use is a 12v dc dry battery.

Employment

This equipment is in wide use in the United Kingdom, mostly with company security guards.

A1 Security Model 62.000 Explosives Detector-Identifier
UK

Weight: 30kg
Depth: 27cm
Width: 37cm
Height: 80cm
Response Time (search mode): 2sec
Response Time (identifying mode): 1 test every 3min

Development

The Model 62.000 Explosives Detector-Identifier was developed by A1 Security to counter the growing bomb threat in many countries. It consists of a portable unit mounted on a wheeled trolley and a hand held search gun. It can be operated for over four hours from built-in batteries or direct from the ac supply. It has two modes of operation — the 'search' mode and the 'identify' mode. In the 'search' mode it continuously sniffs for explosives with a two-second response time and an alarm is given audibly from the probe or visually from the meter. If a response is obtained, the unit is sniffed again for a period depending upon the sensitivity required and the resulting vapour collected is then chromatographed by pressing a button and a chromatographic read-out is obtained on the recorder chart of the instrument. From the results on the chart, it is possible to identify the response from explosive and non-explosive materials. When sifting the remains from explosions, it is desirable to obtain as rapidly as possible, information on the type of explosive used.

The work load in testing samples can be enormously reduced by checking likely materials in the search mode and then identifying on the spot the explosives used. Even samples brought into the laboratory can more rapidly and easily be checked using the Identifier. The Search-identify capability is also a powerful asset in searching operations. The rapidity of the search mode is utilised and subsequent identifications can be invaluable in maintaining efficient operations. The equipment can be used for checking parcels or suitcases, searching aeroplanes or houses and road block checks. In some cases, an overall check in the 'accumulate' mode of a house, for example, can give an indication that explosives are or have been used; the 'search' mode is used second in this case to locate them exactly. The instrument will thus form a valuable part of the equipment of army, police, airport security or explosives experts.

Employment

This equipment is in use in over 40 countries. Precise details are not available.

Below: *A1 Security Model 62 explosives detector-identifier.*

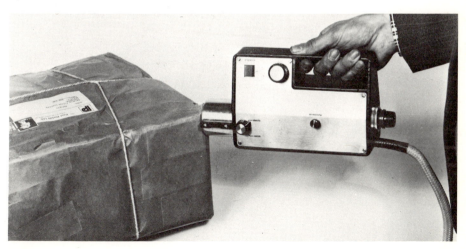

A1 Security Tri-Scan Airport Security System

Above: *A1 Security Tri-Scan airport security system.*

Maximum Baggage Dimensions:
76cm x 61cm x 36cm
Operation Frequency: 5 bags per minute
Response Speed: 3-4sec

Development

A1 Security of Cambridge have developed a combined X-ray and Explosive Vapour Detection System for airports. For maximum security it is necessary to screen everything which goes aboard an aircraft including the passengers and all their baggage. The very high security airports, who are really interested in preventing disasters, certainly do this but mostly by manual searching methods. A characteristic of high security is that a long time is required to search each passenger and manually searching a large suitcase thoroughly can take five or ten minutes. The Tri-Scan Security system gives better security in less time than is possible by manual methods. The component parts of a bomb may not be all in one bag but may be present separately in several bags for subsequent assembly by the terrorist. Use of an overall X-ray of the bag plus the ability to zoom quickly in on any suspect item or non-readily identifiable item both improves the effectiveness of the search and speeds it up. More than one person may view the screen simultaneously, enabling the accumulated experience of several security guards to be utilised. When the lead shield closes over the suitcase a pump reduces the pressure of the baggage chamber by 1/10 atmosphere, leaving 9/10 atmospheric pressure in the chamber. The extracted air is fed directly to an explosives detector. If an explosive vapour is indicated the alarm is only seen by the Tri-Scan operator who can request a search of the suspect bag.

Employment

Various international airports.

A1 Security Model 70 Explosives Detector

Weight: 14kg
Depth: 24.1cm
Width: 54.9cm
Height: 54.9cm
Response Time: 1sec

Development

The Model 70 Explosives Detector has been designed by A1 Security of Cambridge for use by non-technical personnel and has been configured to make it completely field-portable. Commercial and military explosives may be characterised by the vapours which they emit continuously. The Model 70 incorporates a small sampling pump, which draws in air, via the probe on the front of the hand unit. The detection system continually analyses the sampled air for the presence of explosive vapour and when explosive is detected the instrument will give an alarm. The twin detectors enable the Model 70 to characterise the explosive vapour and to differentiate it from other vapours, which have been known to give false alarms on some types of explosives detectors.

The operator is warned of the presence of explosives by an illuminated visual display and an audio signal from a loudspeaker, both of which are mounted on the hand unit. A headset is provided with the equipment which may be used instead of the loudspeaker if the operator is working in a noisy environment, or if the audio signal from the loudspeaker could place the operator at risk. A switch is provided to eliminate the audio alarm completely if required.

Employment

Details not available.

A1 Security Model 55 Explosives Detector

Weight: 8.5kg
Depth: 15.5cm
Width: 32cm
Height: 31cm
Response Time: 1sec

Development

Developed by A1 Security as a cheaper alternative to the Model 70 Explosives Detector, it is specifically designed for use by police and IS personnel. The extreme portability and fast warm-up of the Model 55 make it the ideal unit to use in a 'grab and

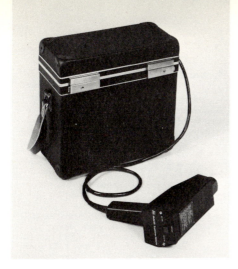

go' situation. The instrument can be in operation two minutes after an alert is received and can operate for seven hours before the battery needs recharging. The battery is plug-in and can be changed for a fully-charged one in the field, if additional operating time is required. Its applications include screening suspect packages or vehicles, searching buildings or aircraft, checking baggage at airports, checking suspect persons for explosives or explosive residues, protection of military or nuclear installations, and protection of vital personnel or key targets.

Employment
Details not available.

Left: *A1 Security Model 55 explosives detector.*

Avimo Frisker Metal Detector   UK

Weight: 1.25kg
Length: 49cm
Width: 5.5cm
Height: 13cm
Battery Life: 10hr continuous use

Development
The Frisker Metal Detector is a hand-held, battery operated instrument constructed from high impact polystyrene. Designed especially to meet the needs of security forces, Frisker's robust but lightweight construction allows searching over long periods without operator fatigue.

Employment
Various UK civil security organisations, and several other governments.

Bonaventure BIS Electronic Stethoscope   UK

Right: *Bonaventure BIS electronic stethoscope.*

Development
The BIS Electronic Stethoscope consists of a pneumatic cavity microphone and a miniature low noise, high gain amplifier. A variety of headrests or earshells may be used. It has successfully been used as a bomb disposal aid and more recently in siege situations where the only means of surveillance has been through the wall of the area in which hostages have been held. It is very compact and is powered by its own built in batteries.

Employment
It is not possible to specify users of this equipment. However, it is in use in many countries.

Bonaventure BIS Postgard UK

Above: *Bonaventure BIS Postgard.*

Development

Postgard is used as a first line defence against letter and parcel bombs. When incoming post is placed on the unit, immediate warning of any package which contains the type of component normally found in the detonator of an explosive device, is given. Suspect items should then be isolated, prior to investigation by experts. Postgard employs pulse induction technology, a principle used in advanced mine detectors. It is extremely sensitive and immune to normal temperature fluctuations but does not require a skilled operator. Dimensions of the equipment are 48cm x 27cm x 16cm. It is normally capable of detecting a piece of steel wire 5mm long x 0.3mm diameter contained within a letter.

Employment

This equipment is in wide use with companies in the US and UK.

Bonaventure BIS 65 CCTV Camera System UK

Camera: 6.35cm x 29cm
Control Unit: 35cm x 16.5cm x 14cm
Control Cable: 15mm or 7mm diameter
Resolution: 400 lines
Sensitivity: 10^{-4} lux

Development

The BIS 65 SIT low light television camera has been developed specifically for coupling to a wide range of flexible and rigid optical probes. The camera is coupled to a monitor screen and the picture can be recorded by a video tape recorder. The device has an obvious application in the EOD field, and can be used to inspect the interiors of packages or confined spaces.

Employment

It is not possible to specify users. However this equipment is in wide use in many countries.

Bonaventure BIS MD2000 Metal Detector UK

System Weight: 4kg (without battery)
Dimensions Electronic Pack:
25.2cm x 15.3cm x 4.3cm
Search Coil: 30cm or 10cm diameter

Development

The BIS MD2000 is not a conventional mine detector. Its two search coils make it particularly suitable for the varied tasks encountered in an IS situation. The larger coil is shown in the photo but the smaller coil, when fitted, allows the device to be used inside buildings and even for searching personnel. The BIS MD2000 employs the pulse induction method of detection. A continuous stream of electric pulses passes through the search coil and creates magnetic pulses which in turn penetrate the earth or surrounding environment. This pulsing magnetic field creates eddy currents in any metallic objects nearby. The resultant 'echoes' are received by the search coil in its receive mode. All these magnetic responses, when added together, produce the output signal which indicates whether metal is present. Bonaventure claim that the MD2000 can detect a steel plate (21.6cm x 21.6cm x 1.9cm) at a range of 87.6cm.

Employment
Details not available.

Left: *Bonaventure MD2000 metal detector.*

Davin Optical IR-Spect Inspection Equipment UK

Dimensions: 38cm x 38cm x 59cm
Weight: 18.7kg
Image Intensifier Gain: 70,000

Development

Originally developed by the Police Scientific Development Branch (PSDB) of the Home Office and now manufactured by Davin Optical, the IR-Spect is evolved from a standard IR luminescence technique used in most forensic laboratories for document examination. In the standard forensic technique a suspect document is illuminated with blue light, which excites weak IR fluorescence. The small differences in chemical composition of inks that arise when additions and erasures are made to writing can create large differences in the intensity of the IR fluorescence. These differences are revealed by photography using long exposures (up to 30 minutes) with IR sensitive film. IR-Spect utilises an II unit to give a real time visible image of the IR luminescence. This means that suspect documents can be very quickly inspected without the use of photography. The IS application of this equipment to check ID cards is obvious.

Employment

Various British Police Forces.

EMI Pantak X-Checker 30 Check In/Weigh/X-Ray System UK

Weight: 750kg
Length: 2.32m
Width: 1.07m
Height: 1.03m
Max Baggage Size: 91cm x 61cm x 35cm

Development

Developed by EMI, the Pantak X-Checker 30 is a combined Check-in Desk, Weigh Unit and X-ray Security Screening Point. The system has been designed to replace the airline's normal Check-in Desk. It offers the advantages of electronic weighing with digital readout, plus simultaneous baggage X-ray examination facilities. Associated with the X-30 is a short conveyor belt. The counter clerk, after ticketing the baggage, can feed the airport main conveyor at the touch of a button. With the X-30 system it is possible for one security man equipped with a single TV monitor to control several X-30

Below: *EMI Pantak X-checker 30.*

units. The system is also marketed by International Air Radio (IAL) Ltd.

Employment
British MOD, British Airways, Cathay Pacific Airways, Sultan of Oman's Royal Flight Complex; Directors of Civil Aviation Kuwait, Bahrain, Algiers, Kenya, Phillipines, Trinidad, Ras-al-Khaimah; Director of Customs Singapore, and US; Zambia, Peoples' Republic of China.

EMI Pantak X-Checker 50 Screening System   UK

Depth: 92cm
Width: 10.2cm
Height: 19cm
Max Compartment Size: 73cm x 76cm x 3.3cm
Max Baggage Size for complete coverage:
60cm x 50cm x 33cm

Development
The Pantak X-Checker 50 was developed by EMI for use as a baggage X-ray system at airports. The system is also marketed by International Air Radio (IAL) Ltd.

Variants
The Pantak X-Checker II X-ray Inspection System:

For baggage and freight this is an alternative X-ray system also developed by EMI incorporating a conveyor belt to facilitate rapid loading. The maximum baggage size handled is 84cm x 53.6cm x 38cm. This system is also marketed by IAL.

The Pantak X-Checker 20: Designed to X-ray hand baggage maximum size 81cm x 61cm x 30cm. Pantak X-Checker systems can be built into caravans for on site operation.

Employment
As for Pantak X-Checker 30.

Plessey Radar Metal Detectors   UK

ELECTRONIC UNIT P6/2
Length: 25cm
Weight: 2.4kg approx (without batteries)
Width: 8cm
Height: 25cm
Weight Without Batteries: 2.4kg approx

LONG PROBE P6A/2
Length: 1.016m overall
Diameter: 3.2cm overall
Point: bullet shaped
Weight: 1.2kg (including cable)

OPEN LOOP PROBE P6E/2
Length of Handle: 1.143m approx
Inside Diameter of Coil: 20cm approx
Weight: 1.6kg (including cable)

TRUNCHEON PROBE P6F/2
Length Overall: 40cm
Diameter: 3.2mm
Point: rounded
Weight: 750g

PERSONNEL PROBE P6G/2
Length of Probe: 40cm
Diameter of Disc: 9.6cm
Thickness of Disc: 2cm
Weight: 500g

Below: *Plessey P6/2 metal detector.*

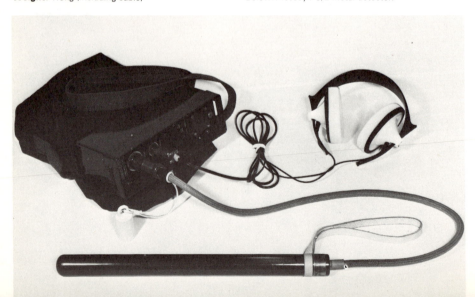

ADDITIONAL EQUIPMENT
Haversack MDA6/2 (Weight 340g)
Headphones MDA2/2 (Weight 170g)
Earpiece MDA7/2 (Weight 56g)

Development
The Plessey P6/2 equipment consists of a waterproof electronic unit and a set of operator-interchangeable waterproof probes. The operating mode is pulsed induction. Target detection is indicated audibly by a loudspeaker or plug-in earphones. Switched sensitivity and response times are provided. Power is from internal batteries or an external source (via an adapter). Four types of probe can be provided as standard, each for a specific purpose. A connection cable terminated in a quick release plug is integral with each probe: P6A/2 is a tubular ferrite probe suitable for searches in bushes, streams and rugged urban and rural environments. P6E/2 Open Loop Probe is a lightweight probe, for ground search applications. P6F/2 is a short robust probe for general searches in restricted environments. P6G/2 is a light easy-to-use probe designed for the searching of persons. Special probes can be designed for particular applications eg the P6C/2 sledge probe.

Employment
British Army.

Pye EOD Stethoscope   UK

Right: *Pye EOD stethoscope.*

Dimensions Control Unit: 25.5cm x 10.5cm
Weight Control Unit: 2.4kg
Weight Headphones: .46kg

Development
This diagnostic equipment has been developed by Pye Dynamics Limited to facilitate the audible detection of active clock-work type fuse mechanisms which may be encountered during Explosive Ordnance Disposal operations. The equipment has been designed to operate in a temperature range of −30°C to +70°C. It permits the concurrent monitoring of a known or suspect device by two operators, a search operator and a stand-off operator, either listening to an active clock-work mechanism or warning that a mechanism once stopped has restarted. The equipment has been adapted and marketed by the SAS Group of Companies and is known as the SA94 EOD Stethoscope.

Employment
Details not available.

Pye PD1 Explosives Detector   UK

Total Weight of Equipment: 17kg
Depth of Back Pack: 11cm
Width of Back Pack: 31.5cm
Height of Back Pack: 45cm
Length of Hand Unit: 35cm
Width of Hand Unit: 10.5cm
Height of Hand Unit: 16.5cm
Continuous Operating Limit: 6hr

Development
In 1972 the IRA in Northern Ireland began using explosives in large quantities to manufacture bombs. The British Army asked the Royal Armament Research and Development Establishment (RARDE) to design a unit that would detect nytroglycerine-based explosives, which were then being exclusively used by the IRA. Pye Dynamics were then invited to develop and produce in quantity the unit designed by

RARDE. This became known as the PDI. The equipment is carried and used by one man. It consists of a hand unit, a back-pack mounted on a standard carrying frame, and an interconnecting cable. The hand unit contains the analysis unit with its associated electronics, and incorporates a display panel which indicates correct functioning of the equipment by means of light signals. The back-pack contains the control electronics, a re-chargeable nickel-cadmium battery and a light alloy bottle containing Argon gas. In operation the probe is placed in areas or against objects suspected of containing or bearing traces of explosives. A sample of air is drawn into the hand unit and analysed for the presence of explosive vapour. A positive response to this causes an audible alert to sound. The alert is available either from a loudspeaker in the back-pack or in an earpiece. Controls are limited to on-off switches for power, gas and lamp display. There are no operator adjustments and effective use of the equipment requires little training. The detector responds to vapour concentrations of one part in several million parts of air. This sensitivity is such as to give positive responses from hands, clothing and containers, many hours after contact with explosive. The detector is unaffected by large concentrations of most commonly encountered vapours such as cleaning fluid, petrol and cosmetic sprays. This results in an extremely low incidence of false alarms. The detector is supplied with various probes suitable for different search situations.

Employment

The Pye PDI Explosives Detector is in use in Bahrain, Barbados, Bangladesh, Brunei, Canada, Czechoslovakia, Denmark, Egypt, Germany, Iraq, Italy, Kenya, Korea, Libya, Malta, Netherlands, New Zealand, Nigeria, Phillipines, various countries in South America, Saudi Arabia, Spain, South Africa, Sudan, Sultanate of Muscat and Oman, Syria, Switzerland, Taiwan, United Arab Emirates, United Kingdom, United States. It is used by military and police, private industry, government organisations, airlines and airport authorities.

Pye PD2 Explosives Detector   UK

Total Weight of Equipment: 10kg
Depth of Carrying Case: 13cm
Width of Carrying Case: 45cm
Height of Carrying Case: 32cm
Length of Sensor Unit: 26cm
Diameter of Sensor Unit: 1.2cm
Height of Sensor Unit: 4.5cm
Continuous Operating Limit: 6hr

Development

Specially designed to meet the needs of industry and commerce, the PD2 explosives detector is based on the PD1 military version supplied to the British Army. It has a faster response time than the PD1, only 3.5sec, but still retains the same degree of selectivity. The PD2 is sensitive to explosive substances containing nitrated organic molecules. Its sensitivity to a particular explosive is governed to a great extent by the availability of vapour from that explosive. Nitroglycerine-based explosives, particularly those containing Ethylene Glycol Di-Nitrate (EGDN) give relatively high concentrations of detectable vapour and the PD2 is accordingly highly sensitive to these explosives. Other explosives such as TNT, DNT, RDX, PETN, etc, have much lower vapour pressures. This means in practice that the PD2 will respond to TNT but to an extent that varies with temperature. It will not respond to analytically pure RDX, for example, because virtually no vapour is available.

Employment

British, Swiss, Italian, Bahrain, Maltese, Danish and Kenya Police Forces; UK Home Office and MOD, Government of Saudi Arabia, Sultanate of Muscat and Oman, and Governments of Libya, Brunei, Romania, and the Phillipines; 13 airlines, the BBC and Netherlands Broadcasting Corporation and some seven private companies.

Below: *Pye PD2 explosives detector.*

Rapidex Hand Baggage Screening System UK

Right: *Rapidex hand baggage screening system.*

Weight: 630kg
Length: 1.956m
Width: 99cm
Height: 1.168m
Max Baggage Size: 81.3cm x 61cm x 30.5cm

Development

Development by International Air Radio Ltd specifically for screening hand baggage, the system uses not only X-ray examination techniques to detect weapons and detonating devices, but also incorporates as an optional additional facility an explosives detector based on the design originated by the Royal Armaments Research and Development Establishment for the British Army.

Employment

British Airways and other international airlines.

Rapidex Metal Detection Gateway UK

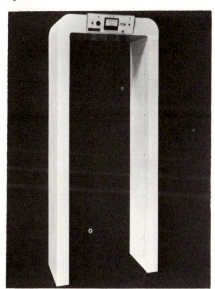

Weight: 50kg
Depth: 45.7cm
Overall Width: 88.9cm
Gateway Width: 68.5cm
Overall Height: 2.184m

Development

Developed by International Air Radio Ltd of Southall, the Rapidex Metal Detection Gateway is completely self contained. The control panel which contains alarm indications, sensitivity adjustment meters and power switches is, in the standard version of the gateway, located in the overhead span of the unit (see photo). The control panel can be sited remote from the gateway if required.

Employment

The equipment is in service in the UK and in several other countries.

Left: *Rapidex metal detection gateway.*

SAS Developments SA93 Portable Battery-Operated X-Ray Equipment

UK

Dimensions Main Unit: 17.5cm x 23cm x 38cm
Weight of Main Unit: 12.5kg
Total Weight of Equipment: 24kg
Penetration: up to 50mm

Development

The SA93 is a compact fully portable X-ray system marketed by the SAS Group of Companies. It incorporates a novel type of high voltage pulse generator developed by the United Kingdom Atomic Energy Authority. The SA93 is designed for use without the need for an external power source, being powered by internal rechargeable Nickel Cadmium batteries. It can also be used directly from a mains electrical supply. The supply to the high voltage generator can be selected to provide four different exposures which give varying degrees of target material penetration.

Employment

Details not available.

SSI Letter Bomb Detector

UK

Development

Developed by SSI of Cambridge, this electronic letter bomb detector is a simple and effective method of scanning mail.

Employment

Details not available.

Left: *SS1 letter bomb detector.*

Calspan Fingerscan

USA

Weight Central Station: 272kg
Depth Central Station: 76.2cm
Width Central Station: 1.988m
Height Central Station: 78.7cm
Weight Terminal: 18.1kg
Depth Terminal: 45.7cm
Width Terminal: 38.1cm
Height: 3.8cm
Response Time: 2 sec.

Development

Calspan Technology Products of Buffalo have developed the Fingerscan system for access control and personal identification. Fingerscan controls access of individuals by identifying them through their fingerprints, not by a card or a number. To request access, an individual approaches the identification terminal, keys in a number indicating who he claims to be, and then places his finger on a fingerprint reader. The reader scans the fingerprint and transmits the image to the Fingerscan central station. The individual's fingerprints are matched with the descriptive characteristics on file in the system. If he is authorised access, then a positive action — such as opening a door or unlocking a computer terminal — is taken. If no match is made, programmable options include additional reading of primary finger and/or an alternate finger as directed. Subsequent unsuccessful attempts will result in an alarm or instructions to call for assistance. A system is made up of a terminal located at each access site and a central station. The terminal accepts the individual's alleged identity number and his fingertip for scanning, and has a means of unlocking the door or terminal once the system has made the match. The system has a military application in a situation where large sections of the population have been fingerprinted. The system would allow random checking of identities at roadblocks and other checks.

Employment

This system is operated by various government establishments and commercial organisations in the US.

Communications Control LBD400 Letter Bomb Detector
USA

Development
Developed in the US, and distributed by Communications Control Systems Inc, the LBD400 screens mail electronically. Letters fed through a gate are analysed for the presence of explosive materials, electrical triggering devices or any other ferrous elements used in the construction of a letter bomb. When the magnetic field is disturbed by the presence of a threatening device, the instrument alerts the operator by two optional warning systems — the LED alert, a silent alarm in the form of a discreet light, and a tone alarm which produces a shrill noise. A calibrated control permits adjustment to different levels of sensitivity. Designed for continuous operation, the Letter Bomb Detector LBD400 can be operated by an individual without previous technical training.

Employment
In use in the US, Africa, Asia and the Middle East.

SE1 FSL-8 SWAT Light
USA

Collapsed Length: 1.372m
Extended Length: 2.44m
Weight Without Battery: 1.14kg
Battery Pack Weight: 4.53kg

Development
The FSL-8 SWAT light was developed by SE1 of Fullerton, California for the inspection of dark areas. It is particularly suitable for looking under vehicles. With its 70,000 or 110,000 candlepower spotlight and 12-volt battery pack the equipment provides a powerful light for one hour (or 30 minutes in the case of the 110,000 candlepower spotlight).

Variants
The 65001 Inspector is 762mm long and weighs only 0.56kg. It is designed for use in confined spaces.

Employment
Various US police forces.

Below left: *SE1 FSL-8 SWAT light.*

Below: *SE1 6500 'Inspector'.*

Section VI: Perimeter Protection

'Perimeter Protection' has become a growth industry since military and government installations have in recent years become more prone to sabotage, espionage and plain vandalism. Intruder alarms provide varying degrees of security. The main aims of a perimeter protection system are to provide the earliest possible detection of intruders; to maximise reaction time; to ensure security against overcoming the system by tampering; to give a low (preferably negligible) false alarm rate; to ensure reliability over long periods as well as ease of installation; and ideally the system should provide protection in depth.

Perimeter protection can be provided by microwave/IR fences, tripwire/differential force systems, or acoustic, seismic or magnetic sensors, or by radar or TV surveillance. Often a combination of these systems is the best answer. Sensors can provide protection in a number of ways. They can detect an intruder crossing a line; they can detect attempts to climb or interfere with fences or walls, and they can sense interference with windows. Additionally or alternatively they can be used to provide focal protection so that the presence of a person in a room is indicated. Most perimeter protection systems are connected to a central control, thus keeping to a minimum the manpower required to monitor them. The more complex perimeter protection systems are computerised.

This section includes some of the more interesting systems available. It does not claim to be comprehensive, as there are literally hundreds of systems available, many of which are substantially the same. More comprehensive coverage of perimeter protection systems would therefore be largely repetitive. Conventional burglar alarms are not included.

Advanced Devices Laboratory Intruder Detector Systems
Belgium

SERIES 64 MULTIPLE HEAD IR SYSTEM
Weight Sensor Unit: 1.3kg
Sensor Dimensions: 12.7cm x 6.4cm
Detection Sensitivity: Detection of person in protection pattern moving at 1 foot per second or faster
Area of Coverage: Tear shape of approximately 6m x 6m

Development

Developed by Advanced Devices Laboratory Europe of Brussels, the Series 64 passive IR system is designed to permit the operation of five remote sensors from a single Model 6400 control unit. The system can be expanded to 20 remote sensors with the use of a 6460 control unit. A standby power pack provides 11 hours of continuous operation in the event of a power failure.

Variants

A long range conical beam-like pattern, 0.75m x 20m, is available on the Model 6401 and 6441.

SERIES 66XX/66XXRM MULTIPLE HEAD IR SYSTEMS
Weight Sensor Unit: 1.3kg
Sensor Dimensions: 21.3cm x 12.7cm x 9.6cm
Detection Sensitivity: As for series 64
Area of Coverage: Tear shape of approximately 10m x 10m

Development

The solid state series 66 system establishes a stable non-alarm condition from the ambient IR radiation from within the surveillance area. Should an intruder enter or leave the surveillance area a rapid change in the IR energy level is created. The sensors detect the change and activate the alarm circuit.

Above: *Series 66 detector head.*

MODEL 4400 LONG RANGE DETECTION SYSTEM

Weight Sensor Unit: 4.5kg
Detection Sensitivity: Capable of detecting man moving in protected area between 7.5mm per second and 16kph.
Area of Coverage, Antenra Type 3011: 10m × 100m
Type 3012: 17m × 85m
Type 3014: 20m × 50m
Type 3016: 24m × 35m
Type 3019: 27m × 27m

Development

The model 4400 has a range of up to 100 metres, and is therefore particularly suitable for long perimeters.

Variants

The Advanced Devices Laboratory offer a variety of other microwave detectors each providing different areas of coverage.

Employment

These systems are in use in Belgium and elsewhere in Europe with various companies. Most Advanced Devices Laboratory equipments are also in wide use in the US.

Hish Watch and Guard Towers   Israel

Development

The Hish Steel Works of Haifa Bay have developed a series of guard and watch towers for use along borders and for guarding installations. The towers vary in height from 6m-6.6m and attachments vary according to the environment in which the equipment is expected to operate. The towers have been used in operational conditions in Israel.

Employment

Israeli Armed Forces.

Yael-5 Fence Intrusion Detection System   Israel

Development

The Yael-5 Fence Intrusion System developed by the Yael Electrical Instruments and Control Company of Beersheba is based on differential force sensors. The system will detect an attempt by an intruder to climb the fence, cut the trip wires or the control cables, crawl under the fence or attempt to interfere with the wires in any way. The system can be installed on any type of existing fence, including concertina barbed wire. An average of 100 to 120 units per kilometre of fence are required.

Variants

The Yael-7 automatic ambush system, designed for field use, detects personnel crossing a pre-determined line up to 100m long. The system emits an alarm, and may be set for manual or automatic triggering of arms, explosives, and anti-personnel mines. The 1.9kg control box of the Yael-7 can be used alternatively as a manual all purpose explosive triggering unit for up to four charges set off separately or simultaneously.

Employment

Israeli Army.

Euro-Med Bv Perim-Alert Perimeter Protection System   Netherlands

	Sensor	CAM 610	CAM 102
Dimensions:	6cm × 4.7cm × 3.8cm	48.9cm × 15.2cm × 31.7cm	25.4cm × 15.2cm × 31cm
Weight:	1.7kg	12.3kg	5.7kg
Range: 8km (Line length)			

Development

Euro-Med Bv manufacture the Perim-Alert system under licence from the Norton Company of the USA. The system is a low voltage system which uses fence mounted sensors to detect vibration resulting from any interference with the fence. Any vibration will break the closed contact of the nearest sensors, which are normally placed on every third fence post. Variable setups for the sensors and CAM (Computerised Alert Monitor) allow an individual section to be adjusted for sensitivity to compensate for local fence or environmental conditions. The system has a remarkably low false alarm rate. The CAM610 can accommodate 6-10 channels and the CAM102, 1-2 channels.

Employment

IBM, Exxon and Dupont Installations in the USA, Chrysler-Simca in the Netherlands, Colgate-Palmolive Gmbh in West Germany, The National Iranian Gas Company in Iran. Perim-Alert has also been chosen as the primary fence mounted alarm system to be used in the current NATO nuclear site security improvement programme.

Right: *Euro-Med Perim-Alert perimeter protection system.*

Phillips LDH8334 CCTV Equipment   Netherlands

Camera Dimensions: 50cm x 20.2cm x 15.7cm
Camera Weight: 2.5kg
Junction Box Dimensions:
28.3cm x 27cm x 13.5cm
Junction Box Weight: 7kg
Camera Tube: $\frac{2}{3}$ inch vidicon
Resolution: Minimum 400 lines in centre of picture
Temperature Range: −30°C to +45°C

Development

Phillips have developed a wide range of CCTV equipment suitable for perimeter protection, but the Type LDH8334 is the most suitable for an IS application. It is fully weatherproof, rugged and simple to instal and operate.

Employment

Fiat Turin factory, Italy; Gas Installation, Groningen, Netherlands.

Below: *Phillips Type LDH8334 CCTV equipment.*

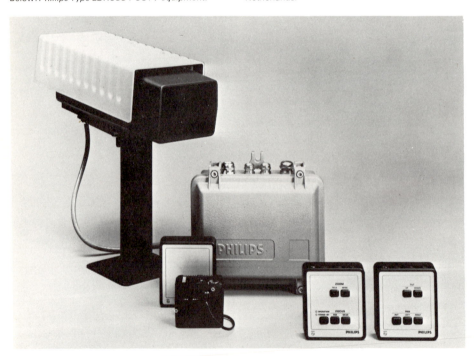

Phillips LHD1130 Microwave Fence   Netherlands

Transmitter/Receiver Dimensions:
45cm x 17.5 x 17.5cm
Transmitter Weight: 10.5kg
Receiver Weight: 11kg

Range: 30m-300m
Beam Height: Fixed at 3m approx
Beam Width: Variable

Development

The LHD1130 Microwave fence has been developed by Phillips for use in all types of weather, including heavy rain, snow and dense fog. The system can be adjusted easily to differentiate between human beings and other moving objects such as birds and small animals. Ideally a microwave system such as this should be used in conjunction with CCTV cameras. In this way intruders can be detected and their precise location and movements established and observed.

Employment

Various installations in the Netherlands.

Ericsson KEK11001 Telematerial Radar Barrier Sweden

Right: *Ericsson Telemateriel radar barrier detector head.*

Sensor Dimensions: 25cm x 28.7cm x 30cm
Sensor Weight: 3.5kg
Range: 300m
Lobe Angle: 11° x 11°

Development

The Ericsson KEK11001 Radar Barrier is designed as a perimeter protection system or for use along frontiers. The radar barrier is a bistatic radar consisting of a transmitter and receiver. These are installed 300 metres apart and are aimed at each other. The units are mounted on a 60cm tubular post. The 11° x 11° lobe angle can be modified for 11° x 18° or 18° x 18°, but this reduces the range by 60% and 84% respectively. By erecting strong wire netting or a perforated metal sheet at the deviation points of the perimeter, the signal lobe can be made to reflect around corners. The height of the radar lobe is particularly impressive: approximately that of a 3-storey building. Sensors are capable of opeation in all weather conditions, can discriminate between human beings and small animals or birds and is tamper proof.

Ericsson also manufacture alarm communication systems to manage alarm systems. The Alarmcom 80LO4 is illustrated.

Employment

Details not available.

Saab-Scania Datasaab Division CSS Computerised Security System Sweden

Development

Originally developed under contract to the Swedish Air Force to protect the Saab aircraft production facility at Linköping, CSS is a computer-based security system intended to provide a high level of site protection at reduced manpower levels. Based on a Datasaab D15 computer, CSS is potentially capable of handling up to a hundred events simultaneously. Alarms, which can be fed in by several thousand sensors of varying types or makes, are automatically interpreted for an operator seated at a central visual display unit, which indicates to him location, priority, provides instructions for necessary reactions, gives break-in progress reports and furnishes a hard-copy record of each incident. The system can also be used to monitor environmental, access and fire suppression systems, and constantly monitors the conection between itself and the detectors so that faults or sabotage are immediately reported. Each change of controller is also authenticated by the computer to prevent unauthorised operations.

Employment
Swedish Air Force.

AD Industrial Electronics Manalert Portable Detection System

UK

Left: *AD Industrial Electronics Manalert system.*

Case Length: 23cm
Case Depth: 10cm
Case Height: 14cm
Weight: 4.4kg

Development

The Manalert system, developed by AD Industrial Electronics of Edenbridge, is a portable detection system. The unit is placed in the centre of the space to be protected, the telescopic sensor is raised to a suitable height which in conjunction with the range control sets the range at which a person's presence can be detected. A spherical detection area is then established surrounding the sensor. The sensor can be located remotely from an alarm system, and can operate for more than two weeks continuously on internal batteries.

Employment

Several police forces in the UK, and the armies of some Middle Eastern countries.

Chubb CCTV Surveillance System

UK

Dimensions Camera Housing:
33.7cm x 11cm x 13.9cm
Weight: 4.3kg
Resolution: More than 750 lines at centre of picture

Development

Chubb produces a range of TV cameras, monitors and associated equipment. The standard CCTV surveillance camera is illustrated here. Weather resistant mountings are available incorporating demisting and screen wipers which can be operated by remote control. Low Light Level cameras are also

Left: *Chubb CCTV surveillance system.*

available. All Chubb TV surveillance systems are designed to provide 'event' surveillance. Either a picture is shown on a monitor as soon as an intruder alarm detection device is activated, or alternatively a 'change of picture' detector ensures that a picture only appears if any change occurs in the signal from the camera. Thus only a blank screen is seen on monitors except when an incident is being shown. This reduces operator fatigue and ensures that the system's components are under minimum stress.

Employment

Various company installations in the UK and Europe.

Chubb Vigilante Perimeter Protection System   UK

Development

Movement creates vibrations and any form of human movement can be detected by a geophone. With a little practice, those responsible at a central control point can quickly learn to detect individual footsteps whether walking or running and also dragging of heavy objects over an area of ground in which geophones have been emplaced. To detect such vibrations, the Chubb Vigilante System utilises geophones in a very similar manner to the way in which they are used in geophysical survey work and in detecting seismic tremors either natural or man-made. The signals are transmitted via special cables to an intermediary channel unit. In this channel unit are fitted special filtering devices designed to eliminate piratical vibrations such as might be caused by the operation of heavy machinery etc. The control room contains a visual display of the entire perimeter with indicator lights to show where the system has been actuated, each circuit has a visual neon display showing the vibrations as they are received and a loudspeaker which reproduces these audibly. One man can supervise a mile of perimeter day and night, under all weather conditions. The system can also automatically switch on floodlights and closed-circuit television. Vulnerable installations can be supervised from a control several miles away and in the event of an alarm condition immediate surveillance can be made from the control by closed circuit television. Geophones can either be installed approximately 0.33m underground or on most standard forms of fencing or walls, or alternatively geophones can be placed in the ground on one of both sides of the fence thereby giving warning of approach as well as penetration of a fence.

Employment

This system is currently employed at Stonehenge.

Donne Holdings Sentry Perimeter Security System   UK

Tower Height: 1.42m (erected)
1.29m (folded)
Weight: 10kg per tower
Power Supply: 2 x 6v rechargeable batteries
Temperature Operating Range: −20°C to +55°C

Development

J. Donne Holdings have developed the Sentry System. It has been specifically designed to provide portable and mobile protection, indoors and out, for a wide range of targets as varied as aircraft, vehicles, petrol and ammunition dumps, warehouses, and equipment stored outdoors. The tripod towers are fitted with pulsed gallium arsenide infra-red transmitters and receivers and can be arranged in a square, rectangular or triangular configuration with the towers up to 50m apart. Such configurations can cover up to 2,500 sq m and can be set up very quickly by one person. When the system is switched on, any intruder passing between the towers and entering the protected area activates the audio siren and the visual flashing lights.

The whole system is powered by integral rechargeable batteries and is fail-safe, in that any attempt to intefere with it activates the alarm.

Variants

The Sentinel System is a more powerful variant working on the same principle as Sentry. It is designed for permanent installations.

Employment

The system has been sold to various Middle East countries.

Plessey IA11 Magnetic Sensor   UK

Sensor Length: 19cm
Sensor Diameter: 3.8cm
Control Box Dimensions: 12cm x 8cm x 5cm
Sensor Range: 20m-30m
Temperature Range: −10°C to +40°C
Battery Life: 20 days continuous operation

Development

For approximately 15 years, the Plessey Radar Research Centre have been developing magnetic devices, including high sensitivity magnetometers of small size and low power. The magnetic surveillance sensor is a low power fluxgate magnetometer with high sensitivity intended primarily for deployment in remote locations for monitoring the passage of say motor vehicles down tracks or roadways, or indeed the passage of any body composed of or containing a ferrous mass. The equipment consists of two sensor units and an optional control box. The sensors are intended to be operated singularly or as a pair in the differential mode and are designed to monitor the disturbance of the earth's vertical field due to the demagnetisation effect of a ferrous body separated at some distance from the sensors.

Employment

Plessey perimeter protection systems are used in the UK to protect government and military installations. Systems are also in use in other countries.

Plessey 3PS Perimeter Protection System UK

Dimensions Drive Unit: 20cm x 15cm x 10cm
Weight Drive Unit: 2.5kg
Selector Length: up to 200m
Detector Zone Height: 1m-2m
Detector Zone Width: 3m

Development

Developed by Plessey Radar of Weybridge, the 3PS is an intruder detection system that relies on special co-axial cable which can be concealed on a perimeter wall or buried in the ground. If an intruder enters the area near the cable an alarm is triggered.

Unlike many beam-breaking systems, detection is effected by the whole body of the intruder, thus giving a better discrimination against birds and small animals.

When used in open ground the equipment can be completely concealed by being buried at depths of up to 0.5m. Irregular local topography presents no problems. The system comprises an electronic driver unit connected to a pair of radiating coaxial cables, each up to 200m long, separated by approximately 2m. The cable pair is arranged to follow the perimeter or boundary of the site to be protected. Movement of an intruder in the vicinity of the cable triggers an alarm which is indicated at a control centre.

One of the cables is connected to a low-power rf transmitter, the other to a receiver. The movement of human intruders disturbs the rf field established between the cables such that an inbalance occurs. This generates the alarm signal.

The 3PS cable pair can follow the lie-of-the-land and does not depend upon line-of-sight conditions. It can ideally be concealed by being buried or hidden behind the walls, and is thus difficult to detect. Cables can be laid under road surfaces or concrete. The cable pair can follow changes in direction and thus the full 200m length can be used irrespective of the number of corners there may be on the perimeter. This compares favourably with systems which depend on a clear line of sight between transmitter and receiver units. For sites where the total perimeter exceeds 200m two or more equipments and associated cables can be used in tandem to provide full boundary protection. Each sector provides independent alarm indications at the control centre without electrical interaction between equipment.

Employment

Details not available.

Below: *Plessey 3PS perimeter protection system.*

Shorrock Microwave Fence UK

Development

The all solid state Shorrock microwave fence for intruder detection forms a flat beam of microwave energy some 2m high and 0.5m thick up to 80m in length. Signal processing techniques detect changes in energy level caused by attempts to penetrate the invisible barrier, and visual and audible indication of intrusion can be provided at a display unit. In a second mode, as a beam breaking device, ranges of up to 305m can be achieved. Automatic level controls are used to eliminate day to day variations in environmental conditions and give stable operation. A portable version is available for areas requiring temporary but effective protection, such as aircraft, vehicles and equipment stores.

Employment

British Police, West German Federal Police, Royal Ulster Constabulary, British Army, Dutch Army, Canadian Army, and US Navy.

Left: *Shorrock microwave fence units and mains power charger unit.*

Shorrock Perimeter Surveillance System   UK

Development

The Perimeter Protection System offered by Shorrock Security Systems of Blackburn are fully integrated systems incorporating microwave curtains or other perimeter sensors, floodlighting, IR lighting and CCTV cameras operating both fixed and pan/tilt/zoom capacities, all forming a system that feeds back to a master control unit.

Employment

Shorrock Perimeter Surveillance Systems are currently used in nuclear power stations, ordnance factories, ammunition and explosive storage compounds, airfields, naval bases, military communication sites, oil terminals, radar sites, missile sites, prisons as well as other sites in the United Kingdom, United States, Canada, West Germany, the Netherlands and Belgium.

Omni Spectra Microwave Intrusion Links   USA

Sensor Length: 22cm
Sensor Diameter: 27cm
Sensor Weight: 2.3kg
System Weight: 9kg
Range: 15m-150m
Temperature Range: −35°C to +66°C

Development

Each Model 300 Link provides a detection pattern up to 150m long and 1.5m-5m wide. Properly installed inside a perimeter fence, the Model 300 will detect someone approaching the fence from the inside (possibly to throw material over the fence) as well as an intruder who has scaled the fence.

Variants

The Model 300A has a wider detection pattern of 0.75m to 6.25m. The Model 305 may be used in conjunction with the Model 300, but is suitable for shorter sections of perimeter up to 45m in length.

Employment

Omni Spectra Intrusion Links are in use in 26 countries. An exhaustive list is not available. However, a partial list of users is US Army, US Air Force, US Department of State (Security), Royal Canadian Mounted Police, US Postal Inspection, Iowa and Arizona Police Departments, and the US Secret Service.

Below: *Omni Spectra Model 300A microwave intrusion link.*

Section VII: Special Communications Equipment

Certain types of IS equipment are an indispensable part of the anti-terrorist war. In particular security forces are not in a position, particularly in an urban environment to use conventional radio equipment. It is by and large too heavy, bulky and complex. This section therefore includes some examples of hand held radios commonly used by security forces. In a situation where these forces are operating from permanent bases it is important that transmissions are scrambled or in cipher. Some examples of portable scrambling and ciphering equipment are therefore included, as well as illicit transmitter detectors, direction finding equipment, and portable UHF Transmitter/Receiver installations.

Radiomicrophone detectors, surveillance tape recorders, lie detectors and other bugging equipment are not covered in this section since they are more accurately categorised as espionage or anti-espionage equipment, which is not in the province of this volume. Efficient radio communications are of fundamental importance in the fight against terrorism. Although conventional military radio equipment may well fill part of the communications inventory in an IS situation, special equipment is usually preferable. This section covers some of the more important equipment in this category.

Radio MF603/673 Hand-Held Radio Equipment France

Development
The MF603/673 hand-held radio is manufactured in France and employed by the CRS for surveillance duties and other specialised missions.

Employment
French CRS.

Right: CRS MF603/673 radio.

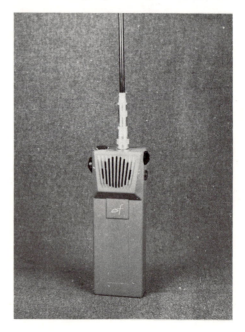

Tadiran PRC-601 Palm-Held Transceiver Israel

Development
As a replacement for the veteran AN/PRC-6 hand-held combat soldier's transceiver (operating on valves), the Israeli company Tadiran has developed a compact solid-state FM/VHF 6-channel palm-held unit, designated PRC-601. The latest version of this transceiver, the PRC-601S, was recently developed specifically for naval commandos and combat drivers. Tests have demonstrated that the unit can withstand a pressure of 4.5 atmospheres without leakage, thus requiring no special precautions for

most underwater applications. At depths of over 45m, special plugs are required to protect the microphone and earphone. The set is also protected against sea water and oil damage. The PRC-601S can be operated when the frogman's head and shoulders are above water. Communications range is about 15km to shore or a surface ship.

Employment
Israeli Armed Forces.

104

Transvertex SR-22 Cipher Equipment   Sweden

Right: *Transvertex SR-22
cipher equipment.*

Dimensions: 24cm x 19cm x 8cm
Weight: 3.2kg
Different Key Settings: 10^{25}

Development

The SR-22 speech signal is digitalised and
enciphered by adding a pseudo-random pulse series,
usually known as a superimposition series. The same
superimposition series is added for deciphering, after
which the signal is converted back into normal
speech. The superimposition series is controlled by
the actual key setting which can be altered by the
operator and is therefore known only by him. The

SR-22 is designed for use in radio and radio link
communications in the VHF and higher frequency
ranges. It can be used on local telephone lines (up to
15km) by means of the SRL-12 adaptor.

Variants

The SRL-12 and SV-22 are alternative equipments
for ciphering speech on local and longer range
telephone links respectively.

Employment

Details not available.

Transvertex TC-13 Cipher Equipment   Sweden

Dimensions: 57cm x 37cm x 45cm
Weight: 25kg
Alphabet: CCITT No 2
Different Key Settings: 10^{50}

Development

J. Donne Holdings has developed this equipment to
interface with any teleprinter or telex terminal.

Employment

Details not available.

Donne Holdings Cypher-58 Cipher Equipment   UK

Dimensions: 48cm x 32cm x 24cm
Weight: 17kg
Alphabet: CCITT No 2 and 5
Different Key Settings: 10^{140} approx

Right: *Donne Holdings Cypher-58.*

Development

Developed by Transvertex of Norsborg, a member of the Ericsson Group, the TC-13 cipher equipment is designed to operate primarily as a static base station. It can be used with all kinds of teleprinter and telex terminals. The TC-13 is programmed using a standard 80-column card that can be inserted or extracted quickly and easily.

Employment

Details not available.

Donne Holdings ITD-1 Illicit Transmitter Detector　　UK

Receiver Dimensions: 20cm x 15cm x 11cm
Receiver Weight: 1.6kg
Transit Case Weight: 7.3kg
Frequency Range: 34 to 875MHz (using 5 different tuning units)

Development

The ITD-1 Illicit Transmitter Detector is marketed by J.Donne Holdings of London. Although originally developed for the British General Post Office, it has obvious IS applications. It is a portable transistorised receiver designed specifically for detecting and locating sub-miniature radio transmitters operating between 34 and 875MHz on the VHF and UHF bands.

Employment

British General Post Office, and several other post and telegraph administrations.

Donne Holdings TRIX Transmitter/Receiver Installation　　UK

Development

J. Donne Holdings manufacture the TRIX UHF Transmitter and Receiver. The receiver contains output facilities for tape recording and the use of lightweight headphones. The equipment has a frequency range of 490-510MHz. The normal operating range of 100m can be exceeded when the unit is sited advantageously. The equipment is particularly suitable for electronic surveillance and eavesdropping in urban areas. Having detected an illicit transmission with an illicit transmission detector, this equipment can be used to listen to the transmission.

Employment

Details not available.

EMI Privateer Type 1313 Telephone Scrambler　　UK

Dimensions: 15.6cm x 9.5cm x 25.7cm
Weight: 4kg

Development

Developed by the EMI Sound and Vision Equipment of Hayes, the Privateer 'scrambles' telephone conversations by inverting speech frequencies and producing a jumbled sound that can be understood only by a person at the other end of the line with a compatible unit. Privateer has commercial and military applications, and could be used at military or police static installations.

Variants

The portable version of Privateer, the type 1314, could have a police application though is probably best suited to commercial use.

Employment

Numerous private companies in UK, Europe and the Middle East.

Left: *EMI Privateer Type 1313.*

Pye Pocketphone 70 Personal Radios

Development

The Pocketfone 70 series of three radios covers VHF and UHF frequencies. The hand-held UHF Type PF5-UH (see photo, left hand equipment) has a single channel, between 405-440MHz or 440-470MHz. A 15v rechargeable NiCd battery gives up to 24 hours operation and total unit weight (including battery) is .482kg. Transmitter power output is 0.5w.

The body-worn UHF Type PF2-UB (see photo, right hand equipment) has three channels chosen from the same frequency bands as the hand-held UHF version, and its operating characteristics are essentially the same, the main difference being the addition of 40kg in weight.

The body-worn VHF Type PF2-FMB is externally identical to the body-worn UHF set and has the weight of .822kg. Its three VHF channels can be chosen from eight frequency bands covering from 89 up to 174MHz and minimum transmitter power output is 1.5w.

Employment

British Army, Royal Ulster Constabulary and various other police forces and civil security organisations.

Racal-Tacticom PRM4060 Hand-Held Radio Equipment
UK

Dimensions: 23cm x 7.6cm x 5cm
Weight: 0.6kg (dry cell battery)
0.8kg (ni-cad battery)
Frequency Coverage: 40 to 55MHz
Mode: FM, Simplex three frequency
Channel Separation: 25KHz
Number of Channels: 6 pre-set channels positioned anywhere in frequency range
Endurance: 12 hours approx

Development

Developed by Racal—Tacticom of Reading, the PRM4060 is simple to operate, having only three controls — a six position channel selector, an on/off switch combined with a receive audio gain control, and a push to transmit button. The equipment is powered by battery cassettes which may contain nickel-cadmium rechargeable cells, or alternative primary disposable cells as required.

Employment

The PRM4060 is in use in some states in the Middle East.

Racal-Tacticom PRM4160 Hand-Held Radio Equipment
UK

Dimensions: 30cm x 6.7cm x 12cm
Weight: 1.95kg
Frequency Coverage: 40-55MHz
Mode: FM, Simplex three frequency (narrow band)
Channel Separation: 25KHz
Number of Channels: 6 pre-set channels positioned anywhere in frequency range
Endurance: 18 hours approx

Development

The PRM4160 is particularly suitable for IS use. The integral microphone and earphone, and socket for connection to external radio ancillaries make the equipment ideally suited for hand held or body-worn operation. During transmission, a 150Hz pilot tone is generated to allow interoperation with all major VHF/FM transceivers and automatic rebroadcast systems.

Variants

The TRA971 Telecal is similar in many respects to the PRM4160, except that it is slightly smaller, weighs only 1.65kg and has only two switchable channels. It is a robust and reliable alternative to the PRM4160.

Employment

The PRM4160 is in use in some states in the Middle East.

Above: *Racal-Tacticom PRM4160.*

Rank Telecommunications 203 UHF Transceiver UK

Dimensions: 20.1cm x 3.3cm x 6.8cm
Weight: 0.5kg
Frequency Coverage: 440-470MHz
Mode: Simplex, single or 2 frequency
Channel Separation: 25KHz
Number of Channels: 1, 2 or 3
Endurance: 9 - 10 hours typical

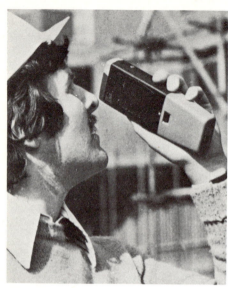

Development

Rank Telecommunications of Brentford have designed the hand held 203 UHF transmitter receiver with built in antenna, loudspeaker and microphone. The equipment has only three controls, an on/off volume control, a three way channel switch, and a press to talk button. The 203 has rechargeable batteries.

Employment

This equipment is used by several private security organisations in the UK and elsewhere.

Left: *Rank Telecommunications 203 UHF transceiver.*

Rank Telecommunications Mitre VHF Two-Way Pocket Phone
UK

Weight TX/RX Unit: 0.275kg
Weight Battery: 0.21kg
Frequency Coverage: 68-100 MHz, 145-174MHz
Mode: FM, Simplex single or two frequency
Channel Separation: 12.5KHz or 25KHz
Number of Channels: 1, 2 or 3
Endurance: 10-13 hours typical

Development

The Mitre VHF surveillance equipment is designed to be worn discreetly under a shirt or jacket using the special surveillance harness. If IS personnel need to work covertly, the Mitre is used in conjunction with a miniature microphone, small press to talk switch, a radiating inductor coil and a miniature earpiece. The microphone, inductor coil and press-to-talk switch are connected by a simple wiring harness, worn underneath the coat or shirt to the Mitre radio. The earpiece receiver has a self-contained battery and does not require any external wiring as it receives its signal from the radiating inductor coil. This equipment when correctly worn is virtually undetectable and has proved its worth in many situations where the open use of radio communications may cause alarm.

Employment

Details not available.

Rank Telecommunications Mitre VHF Two-Way Surveillance Equipment
UK

Dimensions: 13.2cm x 2.9cm x 9.5cm
Weight: .48kg
Frequency Coverage: 68-100MHz, 145-174MHz
Mode: FM, Simplex single or two frequency
Channel Separation: 12.5KHz or 25KHz
Number of Channels: 1, 2, 3 or 4
Endurance: 10-13 hours

Development

The Mitre is a VHF transmitter receiver, designed to be compact and lightweight. The unit has four preselected crystal controlled channels suitable for single or two frequency simplex operation. A slide-on battery pack is rechargeable and can give up to 13 hours service. The Mitre has only two controls for ease of operation, a volume on/off switch and a channel selector. A multipin plug connects to the selected microphone/speaker assembly. The Mitre is built on a modular principle to enable it to be service simply and quickly.

Employment

Various British police forces.

SSI System 15 ECM

Right: *SSI ECM System*

Development

The System 15 provides a comprehensive counter-measures capacity. Some of the capabilities that the system provides are: Detection of secret carrier transmitters (devices which use power or tele-communications lines as signal paths); detection of secret transmitters (wireless transmitting devices); detection of any alteration or by-pass technique employed against a standard telephone instrument regardless of whether receiver element, transmitter element, or additional microphones are employed; trace wire pairs through walls or other structural features in order to determine termination or point of origin; determination of presence of microphone or unidentified wires regardless of type of microphone employed (carbon, dynamic, crystal); activation of microphone detected on wires so that the exact location can be pin-pointed; all components of the system are housed in four lightweight carrying cases designed to protect the equipment, while providing unobtrusive means for movement.

Employment

SSI equipment is sold mostly in the Middle East and Africa.

SSI P-38 Scrambler

Right: *SSI P-38 scrambler.*

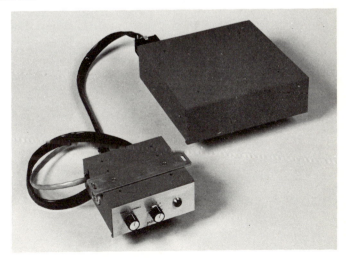

Development

For use with AM and FM two way radio equipment the SSI Security Systems International of Cambridge) P-38 scrambling equipment gives a four band voice splitting facility and eight combinations.

Employment

SSI Equipment is sold mostly in the Middle East and Africa.

Stornophone CQP500 Series

UK

Dimensions: 19.7cm x 7.2cm x 3.35cm
Weight: .75kg
Frequency Coverage: 146-174MHz, 68-88MHz, 420-470MHz
Mode: Simplex/Semi-Duplex
Channel Separation: 12.5 - 50KHz
Number of Channels: 2 or 3
Endurance: 5 - 9hr

Development

The Stornophone 500 range is available for operation in both VHF and UHF frequency bands. The sets are equipped for switching on two or three crystal-controlled channels and have a transmitter output power of 300-500mW. Power source is a 12.4v NiCd cassette-type battery, which is rechargeable about 500 times. Both the VHF and UHF sets can be fitted for hand-held use, or can be supplied with a separate hand-held microphone/speaker unit for extended control. There are 11 alternative specifications in the 500 series.

Variants

The CQP is an advance technology variant of the CQP500, and can be equipped with up to 12 channels. Though suitable for outdoor use, the more rugged 500 series are probably better for IS situations.

Employment

British Army, Royal Navy, Various British police forces, Swedish police, Hong Kong police, and many other police forces.

Right: Stornophone CQP500 in use with Metropolitan Police in London.

SSI DM760 RF Direction Finding and Monitoring System

UK/USA

Left: SSI DM760 RF direction finding and monitoring system.

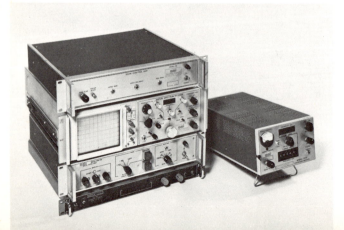

Development

Manufactured in the United States and marketed by SSI of Cambridge, (United Kingdom), the DM760 RF Direction Finding and Monitoring System is designed for Search, Acquisition, Direction Finding and Analysis of RF signals in the HF/VHF and UHF frequency range. The DM760 comprises two sub-systems, the HF which operates between 2MHz and 30MHz, and the VHF/UHF between 30MHz and 1,000MHz. It provides four functions, search, acquisition, direction finding and analysis. The system can provide multiple reception of signals, and scan and search at the same time as analysis. It is transportable in a one ton truck and trailer, and particularly suitable for IS situations in a rural or urban environment.

Employment

SSI equipment is sold mostly in the Middle East and Africa.

Communications Control A-7 Surveillance Receiver USA

Development

Communication Control Systems Inc of New York have developed the A-7 Panoramic Surveillance Receiver to meet the need for a highly sensitive receiver capable of detecting clandestine transmissions of any kind of modulation. It is a portable unit which is equipped with a broad band omnidirectional antenna set which covers the range of 5MHz to 1.5GHz. The equipment has a sweep rate which is continuously variable from one sweep per second or less to at least 100 sweeps per second.

Employment

In use in the US, Africa, Asia and the Middle East.

Right: *Communications Control A-7 surveillance receiver.*

Motorola HT220 Handie-Talkie Hand-Held Radio Equipment USA

Dimensions: 17.8cm x 7.1cm x 4.7cm
Weight: .765kg (ni-cad battery version)
Frequency Coverage: 406-420MHz, 450-470MHz and 470-512MHz
Mode: FM, Simplex, three frequency
Channel Separation: 25KHz
Number of Channels: 4
Endurance: 8hr (ni-cad battery)
40hr (Mercury battery)

Development

Developed by Motorola of Illinois, the HH220 Handi-Talkie is a proven hand held radio ideal for IS use.

Employment

In wide use in the USA and several Far Eastern countries.

Motorola MX320 Handie-Talkie Hand-Held Radio Equipment USA

Dimensions: 7.2cm x 3.6cm x 16.8cm (7-hour battery)
Weight: .750kg approx
Frequency Coverage: 403-430MHz, 440-512MHz
Mode: FM, Simplex, 3 frequency
Channel Separation: 25KHz
Number of Channels: up to 8 channels
Endurance: 1, 7 or 14-hour batteries

Development

The Motorola MX320 is one of a series of five (the MX320-MX360). The five different housings are designed up to eight frequencies, and there are three available power levels (1, 2 or 5w). The MX320 series offer an impressive range of options and are in wide use throughout the world.

Employment

In wide use in the USA and several Far Eastern countries.

Section VIII: Surveillance Equipment

Surveillance equipment is manufactured both for conventional warfare and IS situations. This section will concentrate on the more important equipments produced specifically for IS situations, but will also include some equipments designed for conventional warfare but used widely in IS situations; examples are short range surveillance radars and some weapon sights.

The surveillance equipment covered in this section includes day and night TV systems, lightweight radar, infra-red (IR), image intensification (II) and seismic systems, but exclude perimeter protection equipments which are covered in Section VI. All these systems are an indispensible part of the armoury of an effective IS team. Time spent in surveillance is seldom wasted and often pays dividends out of all proportion to the effort involved. A successful operation is often preceded by hours, weeks or even months of painstaking surveillance. The systems in this section are powerul aids in the IS surveillance battle.

The more obvious systems such as binoculars, stabilised telescopes, and night driving aids are not included. Nor has it been possible to provde comprehensive coverage of all Night Observation Devices (NOD), of which there are some 30 varieties manufactured in the UK and US alone.

Jorgen Andersen Mobile Surveillance System   Denmark

Development

The Jorgen Andersen Mobile Surveillance System is a British Leyland Range Rover fitted out for TV-surveillance with JA1 700 series low light level cameras. The camera is mounted on a motorised pan and tilt unit on top of a three-metre motor driven hydraulic mast. Four hydraulic supports stabilise the vehicle while the camera is in operation. The camera unit and mast is retracted through a sunshine roof to a position inside the vehicle for movement. The system is shown fitted with a JA1 730 SIT low light level TV camera (12cm x 13cm x 44cm, weight 5.5kg).

Employment

Details not available.

Below: JA1 730 low light level camera fitted to Jorgen Andersen mobile surveillance system.

Thomson-CSF Olifant 2 Radar France

Right: *Thomson — CSF Olifant 2 radar.*

Weight: 9kg
Max Detection Range (Vehicles): 2,400m
Max Detection Range (walking man): 1,800m
Max Detection Range (crawling man): 400m
Precision (azimuth): ± 10 milliradians
Precision (range): ± 50m at 1,000m
Power Supply: 12v battery

Development

Developed by the Avionics and Space Division of Thomson-CSF, the Olifant short range portable radar is a solid-state Doppler pulse radar providing an accurate fix on a moving target. It is particularly suitable for surveillance of a borderline, extending the zone observed by a patrol, or surveillance of boat traffic on a river. Although the Olifant can be used in conventional warfare it is particularly suitable for use in rural IS situations.

Employment

French Army. Olifant is also in service with some African armies.

Electron PK545 IR Night Viewer Germany

Development

Developed by Electron of Mönchengladbach, the PK545 Night Viewer can be used for observation in total darkness. Weighing only 1.3kg, measuring only 25cm x 28cm x 8cm, and having a range of 350m, the equipment is both hand portable and highly effective.

Employment

The equipment is used by customs, police, security and border guards and the armed forces in West Germany.

Avimo SUIT Sight UK

Length: 18.8cm
Width: 7.6cm
Height: 6.9cm
Weight: 3.4kg
Magnification: ×4
Field of View: 8°
Objective Aperture: 2.55cm

Right: *Avimo SUIT sight.*

Development

The SUIT (Sight Unit Infantry Trilux) sight was designed by the Royal Armament Research and Development Establishment and has since been developed by Avimo as a lightweight small arms sight for both day and night use. It is an optical sight, and offers an improved target acquisition capabilty under all light conditions by virtue of its ×4 magnification: the variable brightness illuminated pointer, which has a Trilux nuclear light source, is particularly useful at night. Rapid accurate shooting is facilitated at all ranges, the two position elevation level catering for ranges between 0-400m and 400-600m.

Employment

British Army and several other governments.

Barr & Stroud CU19 Passive Night Viewing System   UK

Overall Length: 19.5cm
Max Diameter: 9.8cm
Weight: 1.5kg
Field of View: 10°
Magnification: ×4
Range: 250m

Employment

Details not available.

Below: *Barr and Stroud CU19 passive night viewing system.*

Development

The CU19 passive night viewing design enables a specification to be closely related to a particular function while permitting the user to expand the application of his equipment at a later date by addition of extra lenses on 'still' or 'cine' camera recording units. The system is extremely compact and lightweight, can be used down to starlight conditions, and is ideal for use by police forces, military personnel and civilian security organisations for night surveillance applications. It is designed around the 18mm passive intensifier tubes which are available in 'cascade' or 'channel' forms and only need a small battery to operate effectively for a large number of hours. A simple body houses the intensifier tube, battery and operating switch and carries a small foot which can be fitted with a handle or mounted on a tripod. The bodies have threaded end sections on to which various objectives, eyepieces or recording units can be screwed to give a wide range of magnification and field of view.

Bonaventure Weapon Sight   UK

Overall Length: 46cm
Weight: 2.86kg
Magnification: ×3.5
Field of View: 12.5°
Intensification Gain: ×50,000
Range: 1,000m

Development

The BIS Weapon Sight marketed by Bonaventure International Security provides a passive night vision capability down to sub-starlight conditions. It can also be used for general surveillance purposes whilst not necessarily fitted to a weapon.

Employment

This weapon sight is in wide use in the US.

Below: *Bonaventure weapon sight.*

Fidelity Night Vision Biocular Telescope

Right: *Fidelity night vision biocular telescope.*

Development

Developed by the Fidelity Instrument Co, the Night Vision Biocular Telescope is an II equipment which is available in four versions, the NV50 and 51 weighing 5kg (see photo), the NV52 weighing 5.5kg and the much lighter NV53, now under development, only weighing 2.1kg. The heavier versions are suitable for mounting on naval patrol craft, helicopters or vehicles, although they can be used unmounted. The NV53, begin lighter and easier to carry and hold, is particularly suited for use by IS personnel in urban or rural situations. Horizontal fields of view vary between 9° and 11°, and range is thought to be in the region of 400m.

Employment

Details not available.

Hi-Spy 4020 and 7090 Surveillance Systems

	4020 System	7090 System
Max Height of Camera:	12.8m	22.25m
Max Height (30° from vertical):	7.6m	—
Max Operating Windspeed:	48kph	48kph
Max Headload Weight:	9kg	41kg
Max Sectional Area of Headload:	9,290sq mm	15,000sq mm
Camera Pan:	±360°	±340°
Camera Tilt:	±90°	±90°

Development

Hi-Spy Systems of Yeovil have developed two surveillance systems designed to raise cameras to heights sufficient to provide a commanding view of a rural or urban area, an airfield, vehicle park or any other sensitive location. The mast is raised by compressed air: in the case of the 4020 system this is provided by a compressor pack powered from a 12v car battery, and in the case of the 7090 system by a trailer mounted compressor unit driven by a 4-stroke petrol engine. Different pneumatic masts can be mounted within the power pack permitting greater heights to be attained (in the case of the 7090 system up to 30.48m) and top guys are available to enable the system to be used in steady wind speeds or gusts up to 98kph. The systems are particularly suitable for monitoring crowds, and could also be used for bomb disposal purposes where devices are situated in inaccessible locations.

Employment

Department C7 of the London Metropolitan Police have taken delivery of one system, and discussion are in progresss with a number of countries, some of which are likely to order several systems.

Photo: *Hi-Spy surveillance system* (see page 124).

ITT IR Torch
UK

Length: 13.7cm
Diameter: 6.1cm
Weight: 5kg
Spot Diameter (variable): 1.5-8m at 100m

Development

The Electron Device Division at Paignton of ITT Components Group Europe, has developed this battery-operated infra-red torch. Designed specifically for use with a wide range of night vision equipment, the torch will be of particular interest to military, security and police organisations. The torch intensifies the light conditions already raised to twilight level by the image intensifier. Dark corners, doorways and similar shaded areas can thus be illuminated. The lens system, which can be adjusted in use, provides a spot between 1.5m and 8m diameter at 100m range.

Employment

British Army.

Marconi Elliott Heli-Tele
UK

Weight: 150kg
Field of View: 1° to 20°
Elevation: +25° to −60°
Transmission Link Range: 4-6km (short range station)
40-60km (long range station)

Development

The Electro-Optical Systems Division of Marconi Elliott Avionics Systems has developed the remarkable air to ground television surveillance and reconnaissance system known as Heli-Tele. The system consists of a colour television camera mounted on a helicopter, a microwave link with multi-range aerials, and a number of display units both in the helicopter and at base headquarters.

Of cardinal importance in the operation of the system is the stabilised platform on which the camera is mounted. The platform stabilises the camera along its line of aim to better than 1/1600th of a degree and isolates the camera from the vibrations and positional changes of the helicopter.

The camera attitude and its zoom lens are controlled from a joystick having a two-axis movement. The camera's field of view extends down to about 1° which enables the pinpointing of subjects from very considerable distances. Although a monochrome camera may be employed, the use of a colour system enhances not only the general monitoring of subjects but also the differentiation between subjects of a similar type. If a low-light camera tube is fitted, surveillance under starlight conditions is possible.

The advantages of Heli-Tele are immense for reconnaissance and surveillance in urban, rural and offshore areas. Unit commanders can rapidly survey and search large areas by operating a number of helicopters simultaneously relaying pictures back to centralised monitors and video-tape recorders. They can develop their strategy based on what they can see rather than what they are told and deploy their men and equipment to immediately counter a changing situation. Senior officers are thus relieved of the necessity of making personal reconnaissance. The system is particularly useful in a changing situation to enable decisions to be taken in real-time of where widely spaced activities need to be coordinated from a central position. The long range ground station is equipped with an omnidirectional short range antenna and a directional high gain dish antenna fitted with a remotely controlled drive motor permitting azimuth tracking of the helicopter's position. Antennas are selected by switch according to the distance of the aircraft from the station. The received signals are fed into the microwave receiver mounted with the antenna remote control unit and are displayed on a picture monitor. A videotape recorder may be included with the system.

The short range ground station is transportable and can be unloaded and set up by two men in less than 10 minutes in any convenient building or in the open air. It can also be fully mobile in a vehicle such as a Land Rover, either stationary with the antenna erected or on the move with the aerial down.

This concept of the short-range ground station is complementary to the command post installations and allows multiple simultaneous reception of the aircraft television transmissions by a number of mobile or stationary ground receivers.

Employment

British Army, Belgian Gendarmerie.

Marconi Elliott IRIS (Infra-Red Intruder System)
UK

TRANSMITTER AND SENSOR UNIT
Length: 17cm
Diameter: 5cm
Weight: 0.25kg

MONITOR UNIT
Width: 21.6cm
Depth: 19.7cm

Height: 10.2cm
Weight: 2.4kg

BATTERY PACK
Width: 5.1cm
Depth: 6.3cm
Height: 1.9cm
Weight: 0.15kg

ALIGNMENT UNIT

Width: 11.5cm
Depth: 6.4cm
Height: 5.1cm
Weight: 0.7kg

Maximum Beam Length: 200m
Remote Distance: 5km max

Development

The basis of IRIS is a modulated infra-red beam projected between a transmitter and a sensor; interruption of the beam causes an audio-alarm to be triggered at a remote monitoring unit. Transmitter/sensor links can be used by day and by night over ranges of 200m in average conditions, and an audio alignment unit is used for setting up links when the built-in visual alignment sights prove inadequate (eg at night). Originally designed as a portable military alarm system IRIS, together with TOBIAS has also been incorporated in an integrated civil system known as CIRCE.

Employment

British Army and various other armies.

Right: *Marconi Elliott IRIS (infa red intruder system).*

Marconi Elliott IR TV Surveillance System (IR Searchlight and V327 Camera) UK

Development

Marconi Elliott has developed a night security system utilising an IR sensitive silicon diode array target vidicon sensor tube fitted to a camera, which itself is mounted between a pair of IR searchlights. The system enables an operator, situated in a control room up to 200m from the camera, to observe covertly intruders crossing borders or perimeters at security installations. Other searchlight/camera combinations are available.

Employment

Thames Valley Water Board (UK), other government establishments in the UK, and in many other countries particularly in the Middle East.

Marconi Elliott TOBIAS (Terrestrial Oscillation Battlefield Intruder Alarm System) UK

DISPLAY UNIT

Width: 36.2cm
Depth: 25.4cm
Height: 15.2cm
Weight: 6.35kg (excluding batteries)

SENSOR

Overall Height: 14cm
Width: 38cm x 51cm

Development

Developed by the Marconi Elliott Mobile Radar Division, TOBIAS (Terrestrial Oscillation Battlefield Intruder Alarm System) makes use of passive geophones to give warning of the movement of men

Right: *Marconi Elliott TOBIAS.*

and vehicles, and is effective for border or perimeter protection purposes. It consists of a display unit having four separate signal channels, to each of which up to 20 sensors (buried geophones) are connected by means of wire. The sensors are deployed near to likely intruder approach routes and may be several miles from the display unit. Ground vibrations set up by an intruder impinging on the sensors cause an electrical signal to be sent along the wire to the display unit. Maximum detection distances for one geophone vary with the nature of the ground and other factors, between 50-300m being usual for a single, walking man. Visual indication of movement on each channel is provided at the display unit, an aural display (headset) allows the nature of the movement of each channel to be recognised (man, animal, vehicle, etc).

Employment

British Army, Royal Brunei and Malay Regiments, Australia and certain Middle East countries.

Marconi Elliott ZB298 Radar

UK

Weight Radar Unit: 11.36kg
Weight Display Unit: 8.63kg
Weight Battery, Cables, Headset: 12.3kg
(alternative silver zinc battery reduces weight by approx 6.35kg)
Radar Unit Dimensions:
50.8cm x 48.3cm x 17.8cm
Display Unit Dimensions:
50.8cm x 20.3cm x 17.8cm
Battery Unit Dimensions:
26.6cm x 10.2cm x 19cm
Max Range: 10,000m
Min Range: 50m
Resolution: 25m
System Accuracy: ±20m
Azimuth Coverage: 6,400 mils (radar head controlled from display unit electrically)

Development

The ZB298 Marconi Elliott Radar, used by many armed forces as a ground or vehicle mounted battlefield radar, is also suitable for IS and coast, installation and airfield protection purposes. The ZB298 is a lightweight (portable in three units), non-coherent pulsed Doppler radar operating in X-band.

Employment

British Army, Royal Netherlands Army, Royal Danish Army, and certain Middle East countries.

Left: *Marconi Elliott ZB298 radar.*

Modulux 125 Modular Night Vision Equipment UK

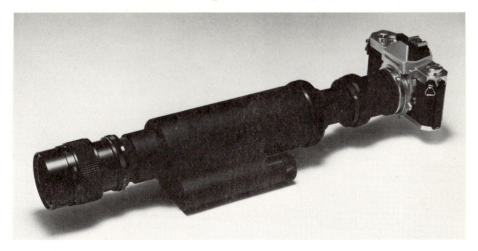

Case Dimensions: 49cm x 42cm x 21cm
Weight: 10kg (less camera)
Image Intensifier Gain: x70,000 minimum
Biocular Lens Magnification: x3.5

Above: *Modulux 125.*

Development

Modulux 125 Night Vision Equipment was developed by the Police Scientific Development Branch of the Home Office to satisfy the requirements of a police force for night surveillance. It is now manufactured by Davin Optical Ltd, of Barnet. The equipment, as its name implies, consists of a set of modules which allows the user quickly to assemble the most suitable system for any particular surveillance situation. Modulux 125 operates at night using only existing scene illumination — to the extent that it can function even when the only illumination is from starlight. This is achieved through the use of an Image Intensifier tube, which amplifies the small amount of light reaching the equipment from the scene by a factor of at least 70,000 times. This makes possible clear observations of scenes which are invisible to the naked eye, at ranges which allow the observer to be unobtrusive. It also allows short exposure times for photographic work. The heart of the equipment is the main body which houses the Image Intensifier Tube and its battery power supply. Provision is made for a pistol grip to be fitted for hand-held use, or the body may be mounted on a standard tripod. Lens adaptors are provided for mounting 35mm camera lenses on to the input end of the main body. Depending on the application, various options are then available at the output end of the main body.

Employment

Various British police forces.

Pilkington Lolite Night Viewing Device UK

Length: 42cm
Diameter: 10cm
Weight: 3.4kg
Magnification: x1.5
Field of View: 21°

Development

Pilkington Perkin Elmer has developed the Lolite-Passive Night Division device for hand use or with cine and single lens reflex cameras enabling night activity to be recorded.

Right: *Pilkington Lolite.*

Variants

The Trilite is a weapon sight designed for use with the 7.62mm General Purpose Machine Gun, having a field of view of 13°, a magnification of ×3.5, a target detection range of 1,600m, and a target identification range of 400m.

Pilkington Pocketscope Night Viewing Device   UK

Length: 20cm
Width: 7cm
Height: 7.5cm
Weight: 0.8kg
Magnification: ×2
Field of View: 15°

Development

The Pilkington Pocketscope is a passive device incorporating an 18mm micro channel plate intensifier tube. The device is designed for hand held military and para-military surveillance duties, and is sufficiently small to be easily stowable in a pocket or pouch. The sight operates in a wide range of artificial lighting conditions and is particularly effective in an urban environment.

Employment

British Army.

Plessey Long Range Man Detector   UK

Length: 31.4cm
Diameter: 14cm
Weight: 5kg
Field of View: 1°
Battery: 9v
Battery Life: 3 months approx
Range: Man at 100m

Development

Developed by Plessey Optoelectronics and Microwave Division, the Long Range Man Detector consists of a ceramic pyroelectric IR detector, and is designed to respond to the IR radiation emitted by a man in the 8-14 micron region of the electromagnetic spectrum. It can therefore readily detect a person against a background of buildings night or day, at a range of 100m. The field of view at this distance is approximately one metre in diameter and the accurate telescopic sight allows precise alignment of the detection unit. The relay circuit can be used to activate an alarm, or trigger a camera, and is therefore best fitted on a tripod, although it could be used in a patrol situation.

Employment

The British Home Office purchased six units for trials.

Left: *Plessey long range man detector.*

Javelin Model 220 Night Viewing Device   USA

Overall Length: 21.5cm
Diameter: 6.7cm
Weight: 1.3kg
Intensifier Gain: ×50,000

Development

Javelin Electronics of Los Angeles, California, have developed the Model 220 Night Viewing Device for use with TV and photographic cameras, and for mounting on rifles. The equipment can be mounted on a tripod and used with a biocular viewer. This enables the operator to use both eyes during long surveillance duties.

Variants

The Model 221 is essentially the same as the 220 but incorporates a focal plane iris to reduce the field of view and eliminate bright lights from the edge of a scene, which makes it more suitable for use in an urban area.

Employment

Numerous US police departments, US Army, US Navy, US Air Force, FBI, Secret Service, CIA, Australia, Brazil, Canada, Chile, Colombia, Ecuador, France, Iraq, Italy, Japan, Kuwait, Malaysia, Mexico, Panama, Philippines, Puerto Rico, Taiwan, Switzerland, Venezuela, West Germany, Zambia.

Left: *Javelin Model 221 and 222 night viewing devices.*

Javelin Model 222 Night Viewing Device   USA

Overall Length: 10.8cm
Weight: .95kg
Intensifier Gain: ×45,000

Development
The Model 222 is a second generation night viewing

device, which, due to its exceptionally light weight, is particularly suitable for attachment to cameras.

Employment
As for Javelin Model 220.

Javelin Model 223 Night Vision Device   USA

Overall Length: 33cm
Diameter: 9.9cm
Weight: 1.87kg
Intensifier Gain: ×50,000

Development
The Model 223 is designed specifically for military and police applications, and is currently in use in many countries. The Model 223 can be adapted to fit almost any rifle. It can be used for observation of the field and for aiming a weapon at night.

Employment
As for Javelin Model 220.

Below: *Javelin Model 223 night vision device.*

Javelin Model 226 Night Vision Device   USA

Length: 45.7cm
Diameter: 10.2cm
Weight: 6.1kg
Intensifier Gain: ×100,000

Development

The Model 226 is provided with a biocular viewer on a swinging door type mount with an optional adjacent swinging door for attachment of a TV or photographic camera. The advantage of this arrangement is that a target can be watched by means of a biocular viewer, and then within seconds the doors can be changed to position a camera to photograph the scene.

Employment

As for Javelin Model 220.

Javelin Model 229 Night Observation Device   USA

Length: 83.8cm
Diameter: 26cm
Weight: 17kg
Magnification: ×7
Field of View: 9°
Intensifier Gain: ×65,000
Range: 1,000m

Development

The Model 229 is capable of locating and identifying targets at ranges in excess of 1,000m. The target can be pinpointed by reading the coordinates on the azimuth and elevation scales on the base of the device. The Model 229 is particularly suitable for use in static observation posts in urban or rural areas.

Employment

US Army, US Coastguard, and other armies throughout the world.

Right: *Javelin Model 229 night observation device.*

Smith & Wesson Passive Night Vision Riflescope   USA

Right: *Smith & Wesson passive night vision riflescope.*

122

Overall Length: 31.8cm
Weight: 1.6kg
Magnification: ×3.7
Field of View: 10.58°
Intensifier Gain: ×60,000
Range: 1,000m

Development

The Smith & Wesson Startron Mark 700 Series 1

Night Vision Riflescope is an unusually light and compact equipment which mounts directly on most modern military rifles.

Employment

Various US police departments, West German police.

Smith & Wesson Startron Night Vision System   USA

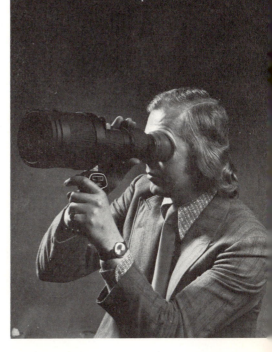

Length: 72.2cm
Width: 39.4cm
Height: 51.6cm (with tripod)
Weight: 27.26g (with tripod)
Magnification: ×7
Field of View: 5.3°
Intensifier Gain: ×60,000

Development

The Startron Mk 606A is designed for long range surveillance, and is best suited for work in a rural environment.

Variants

The Mk 303A Startron is a smaller, lighter version of the Mk 606A and is a hand held rather than tripod mounted equipment.

Employment

Various US police departments.

Right: *Smith and Wesson 303A Startron night vision system.*

Spectrolab Nightsun SX-16 Searchlight   USA

Dimensions Searchlight: 27.9cm × 45.7cm
Dimensions Remote Control Unit:
15.2cm × 10.1cm × 7.2cm
Weight Searchight: 11.34kg
Weight Remote Control Unit: 0.85kg
Beam Spread: 4° in search mode, adjustable to 20° in flood mode
Beam Intensity/Size: 50× bright moonlight at 1,000m for 100m diameter beam
Average Beam Power: 25,000 Lumens

Development

Developed by Spectrolab of Symlar, California, Nightsun is a lightweight high power searchlight designed to meet the needs of IS troops and police, fire and rescue units, and other organisations that require high intensity lighting in the field. The

Nightsun's brilliant but accurate beam is an ideal aid in an IS situation — it can be directed by the operator to illuminate those areas he wants lighted, without creating secondary disturbances in surrounding areas. The high power of the searchlight allows helicopters to fly at higher altitudes thus avoiding small arms fire. When equipped with a special IR filter, Nightsun may be used to observe activities at night without a terrorist knowing the beam is directed at him.

Employment

Various US police forces (fitted to Bell Jetranger), British Army Air Corps (fitted to Scout Helicopter and used in Northern Ireland), and some other police forces.

Other Series Titles

Air Forces of the World
Civil Aircraft of the World
Helicopters of the World
Military Aircraft of the World
Missiles of the World
World Civil Aircraft Since 1945
World Military Aircraft Since 1945
Armoured Fighting Vehicles of the World
Artillery of the World
Infantry Weapons of the World
Military Vehicles of the World
Warships of the World — 1 Major Classes
Warships of the World — 2 Escort Vessels
Police of the World

In Preparation

Police Vehicles of the World
Emergency Service Vehicles of the UK
World Armoured Fighting Vehicles Since 1945
Armies of the World
World Military Aircraft 1918-1939
Warships of the World — 3 Submarines and Fast
    Attack Craft